The Sixth Victim
& Other Plays

The Sixth Victim
& Other Plays

J.T. McDaniel

Riverdale Books
Dublin, Ohio

The Sixth Victim & Other Plays
© 2015, J.T. McDaniel. All rights reserved.

**Published by:
Riverdale Books
P.O. Box 3716
Dublin, OH 43016**

Performance rights for *The Sixth Victim, To Kill a King, Burying Dad, It's the Computer's Fault*, and *Sunday Afternoon* are exclusively controlled by CPC Theatrical, without whose license no performance of any kind, whether or not an admission fee is charged, is permitted. Amateur and professional theatre companies are strongly advised to secure a license before any steps are taken to stage any of these plays, including renting a theater, holding auditions, rehearsing, or scheduling performances. Application for a license may be made to CPC at the above address, or using the links on the company website at http://cpctheatrical.com/bookstore.html. Email inquiries should be addressed to: info@cpctheatrical.com.

All license applications should include date and number of performances, the date rehearsals are to begin, name, location, and capacity of the theater or venue, ticket prices, and the name, address, and full contact information for the person or entity responsible for the production. All licensing charges must be paid in full no later than two weeks prior to the first performance. Any rehearsal to which an audience is admitted, even if no admission is charged, is considered a performance under the standard contract, and must be included in the license and appropriate royalties paid.

Video or audio recording of any performance or rehearsal of any of these plays, with the exception of no more than five video excerpts not to exceed 30 seconds in length for publicity purposes, is strictly forbidden without a license in writing from the author. CPC Theatrical will forward video licensing requests to the author, but has no control over their granting.

Each of the five plays contained in this volume is subject to an individual license. However, if a producer intends to perform two or more of these plays as part of a single performance, CPC Theatrical will allow the combined plays to be licensed under a joint performance license at the same rate as a single full-length play.

Possession of this script does not constitute or imply any license to perform the works contained herein. Copying of this script by any means, electronic or mechanical, including photocopying, recording, digital copying, or any other means, is strictly forbidden, and any organization or person seeking to license one or more of the contained works is required to purchase a sufficient number of scripts to provide one copy for each cast member and each member of the technical staff requiring a script.

The following notice must appear in all programs and printed advertising, and as a caption in all video advertising.

"{Name of Play} is presented by special arrangement with CPC Theatrical."

ISBN: 978-1-932606-42-3

Published in the United States of America

CONTENTS

The Sixth Victim, p. 1
It is 1888, and Jack the Ripper has killed his five known victims. Dina brings a man back to her lodgings. Is he the Ripper? And does she have a surprise for him if he is? 1M, 1F.

To Kill a King, p. 17
This one act play tells the story of the events leading up to William Shakespeare's Hamlet. Most of the characters are familiar from Shakespeare's play, but King Hamlet is still alive, young Hamlet spends much of the play away at school, and questions are raised about relationships within the royal family. The reason Claudius decided to murder his brother makes Shakespeare's play even more tragic. 14M, 2F. Some doubling possible.

Burying Dad, p. 63
Joe and Mary are in a visitation room at Mortimer's Funeral Home, waiting for their father's friends to attend his funeral. 1M, 1F, early to mid 60s.

It's the Computer's Fault, p. 78
Rod is a compulsive computer geek with homicidal tendencies. Lucy is the young waitress he's kidnapped after a personality test on his computer told him the famous person he's most like is the serial killer/cannibal Ed Gein. This is a monologue play and only Rod speaks, as Lucy is tied up and gagged in a chair. 1M, 1F.

Sunday Afternoon, p. 82
Dave and Norma have been married for 45 years. Now Dave is beginning to forget things, and Norma is wondering how she's going to take care of him when he can't remember anything. On this Sunday afternoon, he's just back from the store, where he bought the wrong things, and took three hours to run a twenty minute errand. Their daughter, Judy, arrives and things escalate. 1M, 2F.

THE SIXTH VICTIM

CAST OF CHARACTERS
DINA, red headed prostitute, appears about 25. (Pronounced DEE-nuh)
THE MAN, middle aged retired sea captain. Jack the Ripper.

SETTINGS
Dina's bed sitter in Whitechapel, London, 1888.

SETTING: *A small bed sitter in the Whitechapel slums of London in 1888. There is a large iron bed at right, and an old armoire upstage. A chintz curtained window is above a square deal table, left, with two chairs. There is a metal paraffin lamp on the table. The single door is down left.*
AT RISE: *Lights up, very low.* DINA *enters, strikes a match, and lights the lamp. Lights up higher. She wears a good quality overcoat, which she removes to reveal a rather shabby skirt and blouse, with a faded, patched velvet jacket. She hangs the overcoat in the armoire, and places her hat on the shelf. She takes a cheap overcoat from the armoire and puts it on, as well as a rather gaudy old hat. She then goes back out. Lights go down, then come back up.*

DINA *reenters, with* THE MAN. *He is middle aged, wearing neat but very ordinary workman's clothing and a cloth cap.* DINA *takes his cap and coat and hangs them in the armoire, along with her own overcoat and hat.* THE MAN *sits at the table.*

THE MAN

Nice enough room.

DINA

It's mine, long as I pay the rent.

THE MAN

You're young and pretty. Shouldn't be no problem with that.

DINA

Have to be careful, though. Papers say he killed another girl two days ago.

THE MAN

I read about that. Place like this, they said. Girl with her own lodgings.

DINA

Right. Mary Kelly. I knew her. Thought she'd be more careful.

THE MAN

You worried? Being alone and all.

DINA

Not that much. Might not be that bad to die.

THE MAN

I'd think you would, your line of work and all. Wouldn't want to bring him home by mistake, would you?

DINA

If I did, he might try to kill me, eh?

THE MAN

Makes sense.

DINA

Sometimes I think I might welcome death. Mostly not, but sometimes. You can live too long, you know.

THE MAN

What, how old are you? You're just a kid. Maybe, what, 25?

DINA

I'm older than I look.

THE MAN

Still, you wouldn't want to die, would you?

DINA

Sometimes I do.

THE MAN

Not tonight, though?

DINA

Not tonight.

THE MAN

It wouldn't be right if you wanted to.

DINA

Why would you care? You some sort of alienist?

THE MAN

Nothing so grand. I just care, is all. Pretty young thing like you should want to live a long time.

DINA

So, what are you, then?

THE MAN

A sailor is what I was. Not now, though.

DINA

What are you now?

THE MAN

I do what I can. I saved up a nice, tidy sum. Only work if I feel like it now. Comfortable, is what I am.

DINA

I wish I was. Nothing comfortable about this—line of work.

THE MAN

Just need to find yourself the right man is all.

DINA

You?

THE MAN

Not me. I'm not the type to settle down. No, I get what I want when I need it, and I pay for it, and that's fine for me. No attachments, so I can come and go as I please.

DINA

I wouldn't make a good wife anyway. And I get dead lazy on Saturdays. Never stir at all—just lie around like a bloody corpse.

THE MAN

Oh, you look lively enough. Good for a bit of sport.

DINA

Long as it isn't Saturday. Day of rest, you see.

THE MAN

Saturday? You one of them Millerites?

DINA

One of who?

THE MAN

One of them Millerites. Them people that thought the world was going to end about 40 years back. Some of them go in for that Saturday sabbath stuff.

DINA

No, not one of them.

THE MAN

Just like to sleep late on Saturday, is it?

DINA

Right through 'til after dark.

THE MAN

Feeling frisky enough tonight, I hope?

DINA

Frisky enough.

THE MAN

What you think he looks like?

DINA

Who?

THE MAN

Ol' Jack.

DINA

You read some of the papers, seems like some sort of gentleman, 'cept for what he does. That's not gentleman-like, is it?

THE MAN

You think he is?

DINA

What? A gentleman?

THE MAN

Yes. Proper toff, some say.

DINA

Not likely. A gentleman would stand out around these parts. I expect he's kind of ordinary looking.

THE MAN

Like me, you mean?

DINA

Are you him?

THE MAN

Never can tell, can you?

DINA

I don't think you are.

THE MAN

Why not? I suppose I'm ordinary enough.

DINA

I suppose I just don't want you to be. You don't seem vicious enough. He'd be sort of vicious, I'd think.

THE MAN

Ask my old crews if I could be vicious.

DINA

What, used to give them a few dozen lashes now and then? That sort of thing?

THE MAN

No, none of that. Mind you, there was a few I'd have liked to, if it was still

5

legal. But more than one lazy bugger found himself thrown off the ship in Hong Kong or Capetown.

DINA

There, see? Not vicious enough. If you were vicious you'd have been like the pirates of old and thrown them off in the middle of the Atlantic.

THE MAN

When I was young, one captain I served under, I expect he'd have done just that if he'd thought he could get away with it. One troublemaker went overboard during the midwatch one night. Captain put it down to an accident, but you had to wonder, didn't you?

DINA

(Taking off her jacket and undoing her hair and letting it fall.)

So, you want to get on with it, then?

THE MAN

You mind if we just talk a bit first?

DINA

Long as you pay me, you can do whatever you like.

THE MAN

Just want to talk.

DINA

It's your half crown. If all you want for it is to talk, that's fine with me.

THE MAN

Oh, talk's not all. It's just what I want to do right now.

DINA

You're the customer, eh?

THE MAN

So why do you do this?

DINA

I need the money. Why else?

THE MAN

You're not as common as you usually find around here. Not as common as you make out to be. You talk low, but seems more like an act.

DINA

What, you think I'm some sort of duchess likes to play Messalina and get a bit on the side? Like that?

THE MAN

You've had some education. How many girls around here even know who Messalina was?

DINA

Lots, I expect. She was in that play last year, wasn't she?

THE MAN

It's more than that. You've got some learning. Been to school.

DINA

I can't deny that. I can read. I know a bit.

THE MAN

You're not scared, are you?

DINA

Nothing to be scared of. If I die, I die, and probably welcome it.

THE MAN

You should be scared of dying.

DINA

Can't think why.

THE MAN

You're not afraid of hell?

DINA

Not much. I know what's next, and it's not hell. That's just a fairy tale to frighten children.

THE MAN

What if death wasn't an abstract thing? What if it was right there in front of you? I expect you'd find it scarier then, eh?

DINA

I tried to kill myself once.

THE MAN

What?

DINA

Threw myself down in front of a big goods wagon.

THE MAN

Good Lord. What happened?

DINA

Well, a wheel went right over my head. It killed me, of course. Isn't that obvious?

THE MAN

Oh, having a bit of fun, are we? If it killed you, you wouldn't be here, would you?

DINA

Might be.

THE MAN

You're different, you are. Not afraid of dying?

DINA

Not a bit.

THE MAN

Be better if you were.

DINA

Why?

THE MAN

It just would be.

DINA

I'm starting to wonder if you are him.

THE MAN

Have I tried to kill you?

DINA

Not yet. But you get all night for your half crown, don't you? Plenty of time for you to murder me if that's what you want to do.

THE MAN

Do you want me to murder you?

DINA

Not particularly.

THE MAN

Do you think I would?

DINA

You would if you were him. Or at least you might try.

THE MAN

Only try?

DINA

I don't think you could actually do it.

THE MAN

Even if I was him?

DINA

No, not even then.

THE MAN

Still, if I was him, what would stop me? You're just a little slip of a thing.

DINA

I'm a lot stronger than I look.

THE MAN

Of course, I'm not him.

DINA

Then I don't have nothing to worry about, do I?

THE MAN

No. Anyway, you're not afraid of dying.

DINA

No.

THE MAN

So, if I was him, I might not be interested in killing you anyway. I mean, why does he do it?

DINA

Papers say he's a lunatic.

THE MAN

No. Not so you could tell, anyway. No, what I think it is, he enjoys fear. He enjoys it that the women he kills are afraid of him. Mostly they've been older, except for that Mary girl, two nights ago. She was about your age, wasn't she?

DINA

About. Lots younger than the others, anyway.

THE MAN

Don't you think they was afraid to die? Once they knew what was going to happen, I mean?

DINA

I suppose they were.

THE MAN

But you're not?

DINA

I'm not.

THE MAN

I don't understand that. How can you not be afraid of dying? Especially, how can you not be afraid of dying in a place like this? Doing what you do?

DINA

I know what follows. It's a lot nicer than here. I've seen it many times. Seen a preview of it, so to speak.

THE MAN

You've seen heaven?

DINA

Frequently.

THE MAN

Have you seen God, too, then?

DINA

Not God. They don't let you in; just give you a little taste of it. You're afraid of hell, I think. I know better.

THE MAN

You've seen hell, too?

DINA

Look around. You're living in it. This is hell. It's not a place they punish you after you're dead. It's this place, where you punish yourself while you're alive.

THE MAN

I don't know that my vicar would agree with you on that.

DINA

He might not. But I suppose he's going to be really surprised when he dies and finds himself explaining things to Moses instead of Saint Peter.

THE MAN

You saying the Jews was right?

DINA

Closer, anyway.

THE MAN

So, you're claiming you've actually seen heaven? Is that it?

DINA

I've seen into it. Seen what it's like; what it might have been like for me.

THE MAN

When did you see this?

DINA

Every Saturday. While I'm resting.

THE MAN

You see heaven when you're asleep? You mean, like a dream?

DINA

Not asleep, and more like a vision. God lets me see heaven, but it won't let me in.

THE MAN

You're calling God "it?"

DINA

Best fit. God's not male nor female. God just is.

THE MAN

Why's the Bible call him "him" then?

DINA

I suppose because you can't say "it" in Hebrew, only "he" or "she." Like, "she's a nice house," or "he's a fine day." And I suppose they thought, Jesus calls God "father," so God must be a man.

THE MAN

Never thought of it that way. 'course, I'm no linguist. But you say God won't let you into heaven. Is that why you're not afraid of dying? You think you can't?

DINA

You just get punished for some things. If you kill yourself, you don't get into heaven. Not right away.

THE MAN

What if someone else kills you?

DINA

It's not very clear. If someone kills you before you kill yourself, I expect so. If they kill you after, I'm not really sure what comes next.

THE MAN

How can someone kill you after you're already dead?

DINA

I'm not sure they can.

THE MAN

You're an odd sort of girl, you know that?

DINA

You're not the first to say so.

THE MAN

What if I'm the last?

DINA

What? You letting on you're him again?

THE MAN

For all you can say, might be I am him.

DINA

Doesn't matter.

THE MAN

Doesn't matter?

DINA

I already said, I'm not afraid to die. I might even welcome being dead. You can live too long, you know.

THE MAN

Well, I'm not him. Not if you're not afraid to die. Wouldn't be any thrill in it, would there? Killing someone who wanted to die? Be more like you was just helping them commit suicide.

DINA

What would you get out of it anyway? If you were him?

THE MAN

Well, same thing a man always wants with a girl, I suppose. But, I don't know, a bit more, like. More intense.

DINA

Always that with men, isn't it?

THE MAN

I suppose so.

DINA

I think, could be you are him.

THE MAN

Would that make you afraid?

DINA

I don't think so.

THE MAN

Because you're already dead?

DINA

You can hardly call this living, now can you?

THE MAN

Right, this is hell.

DINA

Close as anyone will ever see.

THE MAN

You can't think being dead is better than this.

DINA

I know it is. I've been dead.

THE MAN

But you came back?

DINA

No choice. They wasn't ready for me then. I still had to be punished for that. For killing myself.

THE MAN

They? Is there more than one god, then?

DINA

No, just the one. But heaven is like here some ways. You got a problem, you don't go right to the queen, do you? You got to go through all these officials first.

THE MAN

You're a very odd girl.

DINA

I'm just so very much older than I look. I've seen too much to be bothered by anything.

THE MAN

Not even if I was him?

DINA

The way you carry on, I might start thinking you really are him.

THE MAN

Even if I was, you're not scared enough.

DINA

Is that what you do? You like to frighten girls?

THE MAN

Feels nice when they're afraid of you. Like you got power.

DINA

Well, you don't frighten me.

THE MAN

Don't I?

DINA

Not a bit of it. And you're not getting your half crown back, neither.

THE MAN

I could always take it. Who'd stop me?

DINA

I would.

THE MAN

And how would you do that?

DINA

I told you before, I'm stronger than I look.

THE MAN

Strong as me?

DINA

Stronger.

THE MAN
(*Taking out a large knife.*)
Think you might be frightened now?

DINA

It's just a knife.

THE MAN

Lots of blood on this knife, girl. New York, Sydney, Hong Kong, San Francisco. Lots of girls all 'round the world before I come ashore in London.

DINA

You are him.

THE MAN

Afraid I am

DINA

I'm still not afraid.

THE MAN

You will be.

(THE MAN *advances on* Dina. *She backs away, but does not appear to be particularly afraid of him, even smiling sightly.*)

DINA

You don't want to do that.

THE MAN
(*Backing her against the bed and holding the knife at her throat.*)

Afraid now?

DINA

No.

(*She reaches up quickly, grabbing his wrist and pushing him back, almost effortlessly.*)
This is why I keep this place. The hunting is so much better than in Mayfair.

THE MAN

Bloody hell!

DINA

I told you I killed myself. In Romania, 630 years ago.

THE MAN

That's bloody impossible. No one can be that old!
(Struggling futilely.)
Or that bloody strong!

DINA

I suppose it depends on your diet.

(DINA calmly takes the knife and throws it away, then pushes THE MAN down, bending over his throat, her hair falling to one side and obscuring the view from the audience.)

(RED LIGHTS.)

(BLACKOUT)

(CURTAIN)

TO KILL A KING

CAST OF CHARACTERS

KING HAMLET, King of Denmark
GERTRUDE, his wife
HAMLET, their son
CLAUDIUS, brother to King Hamlet
POLONIUS, Lord Chamberlain of Denmark
AMBASSADOR, English ambassador to Denmark
OSRIC, foppish courtier
OPHELIA, Polonius' daughter
A PRIEST
HORATIO, student, friend of Hamlet
ASSASSIN
CHIEF COUNSELLOR, head of Danish Royal Council
LAERTES, Polonius' son
FOUR GUARDS
COURTIERS, &c.

SETTINGS

Denmark, in the year 1066–67
The Castle at Elsinore, various rooms and the Garden
Wittenberg University, Hamlet's room
Polonius' House

SCENE 1

Elsinore, the throne room of the castle. At rise, present are KING HAMLET, GERTRUDE, CLAUDIUS, HAMLET, COURTIERS, *&c. Enter unto them* POLONIUS.

POLONIUS
Good day, my dread Lord. I trust today
Finds thee well.

KING HAMLET
Well enough, my Lord Chamberlain. Bring thou
Welcome news? A ship, I'm told, from England
Hath arriv'd in harbour within the hour.   5

POLONIUS
A ship indeed, my Lord, and with it comes,
From Harold, King of England, under seal,
Such documents as will—or so I am
By his ambassador inform'd—answer
That great query which thy ambassador   10
Convey'd to England.

KING HAMLET
Documents, you say?

POLONIUS
Even so, my Lord.

KING HAMLET
Were there no chests of silver carried here?

POLONIUS
Not that I saw, my Lord.

KING HAMLET
Well, fetch him in;
Our tribute is o'erdue, and Harold sends   15
Us documents, the which do please me not;
And so, my great displeasure shall I tell
Unto England's embassy if I see
No chests of treasure hoisted from his ship.

POLONIUS
I shall convey him hence, my Lord.   20
(Exit POLONIUS*)*

18

CLAUDIUS
May I predict, dear brother, what he says?

KING HAMLET
What excuses, do you mean, dear brother?

CLAUDIUS
Ay, brother, so I think. It seemeth that,
In England every day is fraught with peril;
To us they owe a tribute annually, 25
But pay it not, for some emergency
Compels them spend it elsewhere on defence.

HAMLET
Uncle, does England not, upon his subjects
Lay a special tax, the which is marked
And collected our tribute for to pay? 30

CLAUDIUS
Indeed he does, young Hamlet, and he then,
Upon some urgent reason spends it else.

KING HAMLET
Quite so, good brother. Now, you see, my son,
Just how thine uncle in these few brief words,
Conveys to thee the history entire 35
Of England and our tribute. King Edward,
That most saintly man, would swear before God
Some reason why he could not send the gold;
And always would that reason be quite sound,
Acceptable to any thinking man, 40
Yet, I am sure, as false as any oath
That God denying villain ever swore.
Now he is gone, no doubt to heaven's rest,
And in his place reigns Harold Godwinson,
Whom no one calls a saint, but will, no doubt, 45
Again send reason why there yet shall be
No tribute at this time. Think you, my son,
Shall we hear again some bald excuse?
Or is it time to send again our ships,
And so enforce our claim?

HAMLET
                        The which is due, 50
And what is due, I think, must then be paid;
Yet, at what cost? Such expedition may,

The ships to outfit and to man, yet cost
Such sums as may exceed the gain
Returning from the coup.

                CLAUDIUS
               Thy son, I think,   55
Speaks wisely here, dear brother.

              KING HAMLET
               So he does.
Well, let us see then, if we like the words
Of England's embassy, for here he comes.

        (Enter POLONIUS *and* AMBASSADOR*)*

               POLONIUS
My Lord, King Hamlet, may I now present,
Of England's court, this knight, Cerdic by name,   60
Appointed to thy court ambassador,
In Harold's name to speak of policy,
And all things treating on these sovereign states.

              KING HAMLET
You speak for England, then, sir knight?

              AMBASSADOR
               I do;
At least, my Lord, so far as I may speak   65
Within the limits of mine embassy.

              KING HAMLET
How fares England?

              AMBASSADOR
           Less well, my Lord, I think
Than thou wouldst wish. Even as I did board
The courier bark to travel to this land,
Hardrada, he of Norway who doth claim   70
Illegally my sovereign's throne, and seeks,
By force of arms, his overthrow, great troops
Of men had landed on our shores. Our king,
In rightful defence of his crown rush'd off
To meet the threat, and send him Norway bound   75
In hard retreat.

KING HAMLET
                Then fool be he to let
The man escape. Three times did Norway come
Against our land, which we did twice repulse;
And on the third attempt, old Fortinbras,
Then stubborn Norway's king, did we defeat,   80
And lock'd in single combat, we did slay,
So that he come no more against us here.
More than his life, we did much land as well
Take to our realm, in punishment for his
Attempts on us. So too do I advise   85
Your king to do; Hardrada dead cannot
Return again, and freed of him, our gold
Your king may send.

              AMBASSADOR
              And so we would, my Lord,
Were this the only peril to our realm;
Should Hardrada be the only stay,   90
The courier bark which brought me to this land
Would laden be with all we owe to thee.
But more, my Lord, doth stay our hand in this;
In Normandy, upon the channel's shore,
The bastard William gathers up his men,   95
Prepares his army, launches countless ships,
And makes his plans, our country to invade,
Our freedom to replace with Norman yoke.
Thou know'st full well, my Lord, the cost to raise,
To arm, to feed, and in the field support   100
An army to repel one foe, and we,
My Lord, are fac'd with two at once; our wealth
Must first be used in our defence.

              KING HAMLET
                    Yet still
The debt is ow'd.

              AMBASSADOR
              Which we do not deny.
Next year, my Lord, these petty threats will be   105
But memories, and so doth England pledge;
The danger gone, the debt will then be paid.

              KING HAMLET
                  (To Hamlet)
You see, my son, 'tis even as I said;

21

And when this threat is done, some new excuse,
No doubt, will England raise, our gold to keep. 110
These many years our ships have stay'd at home,
No Dane hath gone a Viking 'gainst their shores,
No booty carried off our purse to swell,
But call'd we England friend, and in return,
How little did we ask, of shining gold, 115
Of silver, not so much as friendship's price;
A little cost, to keep our ships in port,
Our valiant men at arms upon their farms,
Our boats employ'd at fishing, not at war.
Tell me, my son, agree you not that here, 120
When tallying the bargain, England hath
The better end of it?

Hamlet
They do, my Lord;
But still, diplomacy can yet avoid
The need for war; send back to Harold his
Ambassador, and with him send these truths; 125
If fighting two invaders burdens him,
Then fighting three will burden him still more.

King Hamlet
Well said, my son.

Hamlet
I've studied of the best:
For you have taught me all the arts of war,
How best inspire brave men to victory, 130
To rally those who falter, and to win
'Gainst foes of greater numbers, as thou hast;
But, as well, mine uncle hath convey'd
That victory may come without the cost
Of Danish blood, by diplomatic means, 135
By words, instead of swords; the same, my Lord,
In Wittenberg's proud halls, I've learnt as well,
As being useful for a future king.

King Hamlet
(To Claudius)
Well, brother, here we see thy peaceful ways
Are echo'd in our son. Dost thou agree? 140

CLAUDIUS
I do, my Lord. For England hath, I think,
Enough to threaten him without our ships
On his horizon.

KING HAMLET
Then to England say we this in friendship:
Until the new year we do give to him, 145
His problems then to solve, his debt to pay.
But when the new year comes, if gold doth not,
Then shall we put in train our fleet, to sail
Against his shores. But rather would we not
Our raiders send, but friends would be, in peace. 150

AMBASSADOR
To England, sire, will I convey thy words,
And then return, I trust, with words of his
As will fulfil thy righteous embassy.

KING HAMLET
I trust thou'rt right, and eagerly I shall
Await his words, — and our gold. Lord Chamberlain, 155
Convey him to his ship.

POLONIUS
                 I shall, my Lord;
A wise king, my Lord, doth in wisdom rule,
The public peace to keep, but still, my Lord,
Where provocation reigns, his wisdom sees
The way to keep the peace and amity 160
'Twixt kingdoms, and to gain those goals he seeks
Through diplomatic means back'd up by force.

KING HAMLET
Yes, yes; convey him hence.

POLONIUS
               E'en now, my Lord;
Come, sir, we shall to the harbour with thee.
      (Exit POLONIUS *and* AMBASSADOR*)*

KING HAMLET
A close run thing, but they are gone.

CLAUDIUS
                     In peace, 165
Good brother, or so we may hope.

KING HAMLET
                    That, too,
Yet it was not of England that we spoke,
But of Polonius; we love the dear old man,
And he loves us, and loves our country dear;
Yet not so much, we think, as he loves words,   170
And to hear himself pronounce them.

GERTRUDE
                    Hamlet,
Go you now back to Wittenberg again?

HAMLET
Ay, mother, that I must.

GERTRUDE
            So soon?

HAMLET
            So soon.
'Tis two more weeks before the term begins,   175
And full twelve days of travel there to reach.
I may be prince in Denmark, but at school
That rank means naught; all scholars are the same,
The lowest form of life. I must be there.

GERTRUDE
It saddens me to see thee leave again.

HAMLET
I am, dear mother, prince by birth, but yet   180
'Tis not enough; I would be doctor, too.
Who would be king must know so many things,
The arts of war, the ways of peace, and all
Philosophy should be his nat'ral ken.

KING HAMLET
Thou canst not stay, e'en for thy mother's sake?   185

HAMLET
Nay, father, I can not; nor wouldst thou wish
It so. Recall that payment thou hast made;
The funds sent on ahead to pay the school,
The which, should I stay here, will not return.

CLAUDIUS
Thy son hath bested thee, I think, in this; 190
What hath been spent is ne'er return'd, but must
Be used as spent, or suffer loss.

KING HAMLET
Hamlet,
Art thou packed?

HAMLET
I am, my Lord, and leave upon the morrow.

GERTRUDE
Well, come and kiss thy mother, ere you leave. 195
(HAMLET *kisses his mother*)

CLAUDIUS
Hamlet, come with me; I have a gift for thee.

HAMLET
Uncle?

CLAUDIUS
A sword, of Wulfgar's forge; 'twill serve thee well,
And to thy German schoolmates will it give
Those honest scars they do esteem and seek 200
In ev'ry student duel.

KING HAMLET
Thou studiest with Prussians, honour mad,
They love the touch of blade upon their cheek.

HAMLET
Indeed they do; but my cheek I'll keep pure.

CLAUDIUS
The greater then thy honour, and thy skill; 205
Who is the better swordsman, he who bears
The scar upon his cheek? Or he who gave
It him? Come, I have it in my rooms.

(*Exit* CLAUDIUS *and* HAMLET)

KING HAMLET
All of you, go now.

(*Exeunt all but* KING HAMLET *and* GERTRUDE)

GERTRUDE
Must he return to Wittenberg?

KING HAMLET
    Of course.

GERTRUDE
I dearly wish that he could stay with us;
He's been at school too long.

KING HAMLET
    O, mourn him not,
Gertrude, his fees are paid, and as he said,
Should he remain at home, the gold's still spent.

GERTRUDE
Yet still I'll miss him.

KING HAMLET
    Well, and we will not.
He much annoys us oft.

GERTRUDE
    He is thy son,
The trait's inherited.

KING HAMLET
    He is thy son,
It comes of thee, not me.

GERTRUDE
    Did thou not say
Of him, his words were wise, just now, when he
Did counsel thee?

KING HAMLET
    Aye, we did.

GERTRUDE
    Take his words,
And from them draw thy policy and send
To England just what he hath said?

KING HAMLET
    We did;
But still we like him not so well as one,
Who was more like us in the fray; a king,

A future king, must man of action be,   225
Not diplomat, who loveth not the field
Of battle. Too long at school doth he remain,
Then here at Elsinore, his uncle's pet,
Learning not to fight except with words.

Gertrude

Thou art too oft away; thy brother stays.   230

King Hamlet

So when I fight again, so shall my son,
And wean him from my brother's peaceful ways.

Gertrude

He is too young; he's but a lad.

King Hamlet
               A lad
Of nine and twenty years; we first did kill
An enemy in battle at the age   235
Of twelve, and counted it a stroke of joy
To see him fall the victim to our sword.

Gertrude

If thou wouldst be an influence to thy son,
Then stay thee here at Elsinore with him.

King Hamlet

To us, it seems, we never see him here,   240
But that he hath his nose stuck in a book;
Like foolish girl he reads, and reads, and reads,
And knows not when to take the burden up
Of future king, when he must fight, not waste
His time with words.

Gertrude
           'Twould do thee good to read   245
To learn about the world and all it holds.

King Hamlet

Thou know'st we cannot read, nor see we cause
That we should learn; we have a chamberlain
Who reads for us.

Gertrude
      Thy brother reads.

KING HAMLET
                    Of course,
He is a diplomat, the skill is one   250
Of value for his role.

GERTRUDE
            Still, could you learn,
And then, when Hamlet writes thee from his school,
I would not need to read his letters out,
But thou couldst read them to thyself alone.

KING HAMLET
What kind of king, we wonder, will he be?   255

GERTRUDE
A wise king, so I hope.

KING HAMLET
We fear a weakling, as our brother be,
Who hath in battle never prov'd himself.

GERTRUDE
His sword is deft enough that thou hast yet
To best him when at play.

KING HAMLET
            Ay, wife, at play;   260
But never once in battle hath he fought,
Nor put his sword to test with death at stake.

GERTRUDE
And yet I would our son were more like he.

KING HAMLET
He's like enough. We want to speak of war,
Young Hamlet talks instead of poetry,   265
Or praises some tragedian's renown;
'Tis but romantic rot, and us annoys.

            (Re-enter CLAUDIUS, *unseen)*

GERTRUDE
Do I annoy thee, too?

KING HAMLET
            Thou art our wife,
Of course you do.

GERTRUDE
Five years, I think it is.

KING HAMLET
Five years of what?

GERTRUDE
Since last you shar'd my bed.   270

KING HAMLET
Thou art old.

GERTRUDE
Thou art older.

KING HAMLET
We wear it
More lightly than thou dost.

GERTRUDE
Still I have needs.

KING HAMLET
We gave to thee a son.

GERTRUDE
And since that day,
Since nine and twenty years, hath hardly tried
To get from me another.

KING HAMLET
Are we not   275
A loving husband?

GERTRUDE
Even so, whene'er
The public's eye be on us both. Ne'er else.

KING HAMLET
We made of thee a queen, gave thee honour,
Set thee on a throne, set thee above
All Danish womanhood in power. What else?   280

GERTRUDE
And love?

KING HAMLET
We did marry thee, did we not?

GERTRUDE
I wonder if thou didst. Didst marry me?
Didst marry countess? didst marry county?
Wert thou entrancéd by my youth when first
We met? Or didst thou say, 'should I take her   285
To bride, I'll Storstrum gain. She's rich and young,
Nor hath her father any heir but she.'
Tell me, Hamlet, which it was. Which took thee?

KING HAMLET
You know that it was thee.

GERTRUDE
    It was?

KING HAMLET
        Of course;
For without thee I'd ne'er have got the land.   290

GERTRUDE
My loving mother was in this a liar,
For she did say that for thee love would grow,
Since she did not my father know before
That day they wed, yet was her love for him
So deep and strong her veneration was   295
For him alone.

KING HAMLET
    Thy mother was a shrew.

GERTRUDE
To thee, who well deserve it, so she was.
When still a child, young Hamlet was my joy,
And for thou wast his sire, I love'd thee, too;
Yet on his day of birth, so far away   300
Wert thou that full week passéd ere thou knew.

KING HAMLET
'Twas our task to get him, thine to bear him;
Now, for the getting must we then be there,
But for the bearing, then we're needed not,
And could that day kill Fortinbras instead.   305

GERTRUDE
Thy generals were competent enough,
And would have kill'd him for thee just as well,
Hadst thou stay'd home to welcome here thy son.

King Hamlet
Of Fortinbras or birthing 'twas our joy
That old king to slay. To take the field, or 310
Stay with thee? The fighting I prefer must
Be upon the field of battle. Thou art
Too common, though of noble birth; art old,
Yet wish the pleasures of the marriage bed,
Dried up, infertile though thou art, how then 315
Doth carnal ecstasy to thee appeal?

Gertrude
Yet still it does, to me, if not to thee;
Rather wouldst thou a swinish souse be found,
Carousing with thy soldiers, not with me.

King Hamlet
They are more interesting than thee, old wife; 320
Much would I rather be at war than here.

Gertrude
Then go and fight another; who can say,
Perhaps I shall be lucky and you'll die.

King Hamlet
What then of thee? What wouldst thou do?

Gertrude
                      I'ld play
The merry widow; another husband find. 325

King Hamlet
Yet none, we think, would have thee at thy age;
Thou art dried up and barren of old age,
No dowry couldst thou bring, no land at all,
For that which was thy father's now is mine,
And will be Hamlet's when I die, not thine. 330

Gertrude
Abominable swine, I hate thee so.

King Hamlet
Hush now, someone comes.

(Enter Polonius*)*

POLONIUS
                    England's envoy,
My Lord, departed with the tide.

KING HAMLET
                    Good news,
We hope, he'll bring on his return; the threat
We made to England was sincere, but yet,   335
Our borders, also, now are under threat,
And England's words are true, the cost is great
To put an army in the field, or e'en
A garrison to feed.

POLONIUS
                    I trust, my Lord,
What next we hear from England will at last,   340
Bring news of tributes honoured, not in breach;
Thy offer of protection must, I think,
Be there receivéd in its honest light,
And Harold, in his wisdom, shall agree,
The tribute send, and sanction of thee lift.   345

GERTRUDE
What of our son, good Polonius? Hath
He departed hence?

POLONIUS
On the morrow, my Lady, so he said,
My young Lord shall depart for Wittenberg.

GERTRUDE
I'll to him now before he leaves. I beg   350
Thy leave, my Lord.

KING HAMLET
                    Go. Our blessing give him.
              (*Exit* GERTRUDE)
Lord Chamberlain, I pray thee, leave us now;
We would devote a time to thought.

POLONIUS
                    My Lord,
Humbly do I take my leave of thee, and
May God's blessings always bring thee peace.   355

(*Exit* POLONIUS)

King Hamlet

Peace? What care I for peace? 'Tis war I love,
Not wasting here in Frigga's homely bliss;
The trumpet doth compel me to the field,
The martial drum, the clash of steel on steel,
Sweet music to the soldier's valiant heart. 360
What woman e'er can lift my spirit so?
O, Gertrude, thirty years have we in twain
Been harnessèd together, and in all
Those years my love for thee remains unchang'd;
When wed I lov'd thee not; nor do I now. 365
Considerations of the dynast sort
Compell'd our marriage, asked of thee a son,
The which thou didst produce, and name'd for me,
And wouldst thou had been satisfied with him,
And kept thee from my bed for all time since. 370
What is a queen, but God's appointed way
For present king to get another king;
Why should king care at all for queen or wife?
We are actors, nothing more; our subjects
Are our audience, there to watch us play, 375
Applaud our skill as 'cross the stage we tread,
And for that audience we do love our queen,
Such they expect, and expectations met,
It matters not what's hid from public eye.
Love is love, and land is land, and land doth last 380
When love hath fled the scene. Land outlasts life,
For land may be bequeath'd, but life can not.
Now, to our son, we two are still in love,
For he loves her, and me as well, and so
I love his mother, love when he can see, 385
For though it be illusion it doth aid
To keep the peace within the family;
He is my son, my heir, and one day may,
Upon my throne be seated, guardian
To all my legacy, and I would wish, 390
Should some dispute arise, to keep my son
Always upon my side. As for Gertrude,
She did provide the son, kept hope alive,
That yet, for one more generation, we
Shall rule in Denmark, though I think it sad, 395
That giving birth could not have ta'en her life;
It should be different, I think, had I
Been full in charge in raising up the boy,
Put sword, not book, in hand, forg'd warrior,

Not scholar: 'tis leadership in battle
That makes the king.
(Enter OSRIC)
Good Osric! here at last!

OSRIC
My horse, alas, my Lord, was obstinate,
Else I had galloped faster to comply
With thy most welcome summons.

KING HAMLET
We have, my friend,
A gift for thee, one we think most welcome;
There is a parcel, two hundred acres,
Upon the eastern border of thy land;
Now do we give it thee, together with
Six families thereon, and all their rents.

OSRIC
I live to serve your majesty, no gifts
Do I require.

KING HAMLET
Wilt thou refuse us this,
To make thee richer and reward thy trust?

OSRIC
I would not, for the world, refuse thy gift,
But only say, my loyalty's not bought,
I would be faithful unto thee though poor.

KING HAMLET
How much the more then, when in wealth thou dwell'st.

OSRIC
Indeed, my Lord.

KING HAMLET
And so the land is thine.

OSRIC
Most gracious sovereign, all that's mine is thine.

KING HAMLET
May we, then, ask of thee a boon, my friend?

OSRIC

Of course, my Lord. 420

KING HAMLET

We have, of late, suffer'd much of boredom,
The cure for which, we think, is exercise;
Hast brought thy sword with thee?

OSRIC

I have, my Lord.

KING HAMLET

Perhaps you'll draw then? Fight a bout with us?

OSRIC

I should be greatly honour'd, good my Lord; 425
At thy disposal shall I place my sword,
My poor, weak sword, which is no match for thine.

KING HAMLET

Then come, our private chamber is, we think,
Most fit a place to fight our little bout.

(Exeunt KING HAMLET *with* OSRIC. CLAUDIUS *takes stage)*

CLAUDIUS

So, brother, deep in thought thou seem'd to be, 430
I wonder what it was thou ponder'd on?
Why dost thou dally, brother, with that man,
When wife so fair and lovely would be thine?
It is not right, that fair one to neglect.
Well, thus it is, and I can but accept, 435
There's naught can do to remedy the fault.

(Exit CLAUDIUS*)*

SCENE 2

A public room in the castle, a few months later.
Enter GERTRUDE *with* CLAUDIUS, *Gertrude*
reading a letter.

GERTRUDE
(*Reading*)
'The work here is very intense, and there is plenty of it. I have very little time to rest; none at all for recreation. My friend Horatio says I work too hard. I wonder, dear mother, if he works hard enough. Yet is he a good friend and companion. My studies call, and the learned doctors here are most insistent all is done on time. Let me then say "adieu," dear mother. My love to thee, and all at Elsinore. Hamlet.'

CLAUDIUS
It seems he wants not for work.

GERTRUDE
     How wonderful   10
It is to me when that he writes to me;
The bleak and lonely life at Elsinore
Is much relievéd by his welcome words.

CLAUDIUS
He'll soon enough return, and stay this time,
For when this final term be done they shall,   15
In solemn rite award this last degree,
Dub him a doctor of philosophy.

GERTRUDE
Swiftly may it come: thy brother is more calm,
Far easier to live with when at home
Our son doth dwell, as if, in being here   20
The son doth calm the father, or, perhaps,
The father calms himself to hide himself,
Pretending love he shows not when alone.

CLAUDIUS
My brother is a man most difficult,
Of fiery temper, and a warrior,   25
Yet still he is, I think, a goodly king.

GERTRUDE
For Denmark he may be; though not for me.

CLAUDIUS
Could I, I would rebuke him for the way
He speaks and acts when none are near at hand,
For the dismissive manner he adopts 30
With thee, ay, and, indeed, for all the hurt
Thou suffer'st at his hand. Yet I may not
Rebuke him, for king is king, and all must
Bow before the office, how e'er so vile the man.

GERTRUDE
Rememb'rest thou the day we first did meet? 35

CLAUDIUS
O, well indeed. The count, thy father there,
Thy mother at his side, and both array'd
In all their finest as they came to court,
To bring thee here, as it had been arrang'd,
And wed thee to my brother, future king. 40

GERTRUDE
I well recall, for I was terrified;
So when I saw thy brother standing there,
And thee beside him, both of you so young,
And with thou twain, thy father, looking grim.

CLAUDIUS
So did he oft, look grim, yet never was. 45

GERTRUDE
So true.

CLAUDIUS
He was a loving gentleman,
For all his stern and threat'ning countenance.
Recall you, when my mother died, how he,
As if his grief were tangible, so soon
Himself began to waste away, to die, 50
As loss of well lov'd wife depriv'd his soul
Of animative force.

GERTRUDE
I still recall,
When first I saw two brothers standing there,
The way my heart leapt in my wary breast,
And though my mother said that love would come, 55
Would grow and flourish only once we'd wed,

I thought her wrong, that love was there at once;
At least, until thy brother came to me,
When I did realise affairs of state,
Take precedence above affairs of love, 60
For princes choose their loves for what they bring,
And treaty and dynastic claims o'er-rule
A woman's choice of brothers. So I saw,
So duty push'd aside my love for thee,
And wed me fast to Hamlet, as his queen. 65

CLAUDIUS
The day will come, good Gertrude, when thy son
Shall rule in Denmark.

GERTRUDE
That day I'll rejoice,
For it will mean my husband no more lives.

CLAUDIUS
Do not say that.

GERTRUDE
Dost thou recall the night, one year about, 70
From when I first was wed?

CLAUDIUS
I fear I do.

GERTRUDE
The full moon gleaming o'er the harbour's glass,
The gentle breeze, the night birds' song, and thee,
So young and handsome there.

CLAUDIUS
And, O, so drunk!

GERTRUDE
So were we both that night. 75

CLAUDIUS
Wiser now, I hope.

GERTRUDE
You've never married.

CLAUDIUS
And doubtless never shall.

GERTRUDE
I'd marry thee.

CLAUDIUS
Speak not of foolish things; thou art not free,
Nor is it safe to contemplate such things;
Thou hast a husband, and we have our heads,   80
Which he should separate from us at once
Were he to hear thee speak of this at all.

GERTRUDE
I would I had him not.

CLAUDIUS
As so would I,
But Hamlet is a vigorous, strong man,
He shall, I think, outlive the both of us,   85
As oft we see in those deserve it least.

GERTRUDE
Then should we hope for war, for in the fight
Some enemy may take him off for us.

CLAUDIUS
To no avail, for though I care for thee,
And thee for me, thou art my brother's wife,   90
And brother may not marry brother's wife,
Except some bishop, or some king, permit;
No bishop would, and should thy husband die
Thy son will be the king, and though his love
For both of us be strong, I think he would   95
Be moralist in this.

GERTRUDE
My happiness,
Methinks, would be his wish.

CLAUDIUS
I doubt it much.

GERTRUDE
He favours thee, I think, above the king;
He's very like thee in the way he thinks,
His gentleness contrasts with Hamlet's rage,   100
His peaceful soul 'gainst father's warlike ways.

CLAUDIUS
Still would he not approve were we both free.

GERTRUDE
I wonder still, is he his father's son?

CLAUDIUS
About such things we must not speculate.

GERTRUDE
'Twas at the proper time.

CLAUDIUS
                Thy head doth rest   105
Securely on thy neck, and 'tis my wish
To see it so remain. Thou canst not let
Thy husband e'er suspect his heir be not his own.

GERTRUDE
Yet still I think he's thine.

CLAUDIUS
              Think if you will,
But say it not to anyone at all.   110

GERTRUDE
Thou art wise; I wish that I were as well.

CLAUDIUS
Whatever wisdom I possess is thine,
If thou but ask it; so wisdom's counsel is,
Whatever thou may'st think say naught at all.
Thy son returneth soon, so take from that   115
Thy consolation.

GERTRUDE
            Though it be so soon,
Yet cannot ever it be soon enough.

(Exeunt)

SCENE 3

Wittenberg, HAMLET's chamber. Enter HAMLET and HORATIO, carrying books. HAMLET takes a letter from the table.

HORATIO
Old Hartenstein, methinks, doth love to hear
The echoes of his voice within the hall;
He lectures without end and I grow bored.

HAMLET
Still rather would I hear him rattle on,
And shake the rafters with his whistling voice, 5
Than parse a page of Cicero instead.
    (*Opening the letter*)
Besides, his dull verbosity recalls
Our chamberlain at home, and so doth this.

HORATIO
'Tis from your chamberlain?

HAMLET
    Nay, his daughter.

HORATIO
What does she say, my Lord?

HAMLET
    That all are well, 10
My mother and my father both do thrive,
Her father still as tedious as ere wast,
Her brother is reported also well,
But she complains his letters are too scarce,
And wonders if in Paris he doth stray 15
From chastity.

HORATIO
  I would.

HAMLET
    And Osric now
Is made a count, a strange event for sure,
I wonder why my father would do thus,
For sure he is an idiot no doubt.

HORATIO
Thy father?

HAMLET
        Osric. A foolish, flighty,   20
Gaudy sort of man of little use,
Methinks, in any enterprise, but yet
My father honours him, I know not why.

HORATIO
What of your correspondent? is she fair?

HAMLET
In Denmark, where beauty is always found,   25
The fair Ophelia sets the standard there.

HORATIO
Is romance to be found there, good my Lord?

HAMLET
If I were free to choose, there well might be;
For she is fair, and gentle in her ways,
And would, methinks, a good companion be.   30
Her dower, though, would not be large at all,
For though her father's office be most high,
Of wealth and land, he hath not very much;
So would my father frown on such a match,
Which brings not gold nor land, but only love.   35

HORATIO
What more is there, my Lord, than love? It is
The fashion of the age, so minstrels say.

HAMLET
Dost thou love Eva, good Horatio?
Thou seem'st to woo her much, when she thy ale
Doth set before thee under Three Crowns' roof.   40

HORATIO
Quite pleasant company, but not for life.

HAMLET
Then best beware her father: I do think
He sees in thee the makings of a son,
For though thou art not rich as some may be,
Still is thy father knight, with fertile lands,   45
And gold enough to send thee here to school.

HORATIO
Peace, my Lord, for rivals have I many,
The girl is lovely, wanting not for swains.

HAMLET
And of them thou art richest, so 'tis clear,
Her father shall attach most worth to thee, 50
Til there thou stand'st, and girl and priest attend,
Her father witness jointly with his axe.

HORATIO
Wouldst thou have me be as thee in this,
My choice the hostage to my gentle state,
No voice at all to whom I'll wedded be, 55
Forsaking love for mercenary whims,
My fate decided by some other's goals?

HAMLET
I merely counsel caution, my good friend.

HORATIO
It could the worser be; sweet Eva is,
As thou must surely know, a winsome lass, 60
With hair of purest gold, and so sweet face,
Her figure slim and svelte where should be slim,
Yet plump and fair where plump and fair should be.

HAMLET
I prithee, good Horatio, think more clear,
For know you not, the maid, so beautiful, 65
Becomes, some few years hence, her mother's twin?

HORATIO
Then shall I to the inn, my Lord, to see,
Where image of sweet Eva as she is,
May wipe away the image in my mind,
Whereon thou hast so rudely writ her mother. 70

(Exit HORATIO *)*

HAMLET
Be wary then, my friend. So now, to thee,
Ophelia, what shall I write?

(Exit)

SCENE 4

> *Elsinore. A hall in the castle. Enter* CLAUDIUS, *reading. Enter to him a* PRIEST, *much distracted.*

CLAUDIUS
Good day, good father.

PRIEST
My Lord, good even.

CLAUDIUS
So soon? Methought it still the afternoon.

PRIEST
Not so, my Lord, the vesper bell hath struck.

CLAUDIUS
My mind was elsewhere occupied, I think.
Tell me, good father, do I know thee here? 5

PRIEST
Nay, my Lord, I am but new arrivéd
To this town, and serve the parish of Saint
Katherine.

CLAUDIUS
What brings thee to the castle
Then this day?

PRIEST
My Lord, I dare not tell thee;
For that which beareth sacramental seal, 10
May then be known to God, but no one else.

CLAUDIUS
Confession's seal, I doubt you mean, by this.

PRIEST
Confession, so it is, and priest in pain;
For that call'd man within me doth protest
That secrets such as this should ne'er be kept, 15
Yet priest and God say that they always must.

CLAUDIUS
Thou dost not like the thing this soul hath done?

PRIEST
Or will do, but I cannot speak of it.

CLAUDIUS
What course, then, must thou take? The bishop tell?
Confession of thine own?

PRIEST
I'll hold all in, 20
It is the only course.

CLAUDIUS
I shall presume,
Whatever hath been said, to me means naught,
Nor doth it touch my life?

PRIEST
Not so I think,
My Lord. Nay, not directly so.

CLAUDIUS
If so,
Wouldst thou in some way say, or still keep mute? 25

PRIEST
My Lord, were there some threat to thee, be sure
That I would find some way to warn thee,
Though it be round about and ne'er spoke straight;
No danger threatens thee beyond that peril,
Which threatens man through all his days of life. 30

CLAUDIUS
I thank thee, Father, for thy warranty.

PRIEST
I wonder, hast thou seen the queen, my Lord?

CLAUDIUS
But yesterday.

PRIEST
Didst find her healthy then?

CLAUDIUS
In most excellent health, methinks she was.

PRIEST
'Tis given out, my Lord, she may be ill.   35

CLAUDIUS
I saw no sign.

PRIEST
So sudden illness comes,
That one may yet retire in perfect health,
And on the morrow not awake at all.

CLAUDIUS
There's something in these words I do not like.

PRIEST
I may have said too much, but, good my Lord,   40
The prudent man might, for no reason said,
Keep watch upon that lady's chamber door
Throughout this night, and keep contagion out.

CLAUDIUS
I thank thee greatly for this sage advice.
But, father, say, who didst thou hear this day,   45
Within the closet of thy shriving booth?

PRIEST
My Lord, the voice I knoweth not, nor what,
In full, was there confess'd to me this day,
But merely urge some caution for the queen,
That no contagion come to her by night.   50

CLAUDIUS
So shall I remember, honest priest.
            (*Exit* PRIEST)
Contagion comes by night, or so thou say'st,
Yet may not come at all if guarded well;
Who told thee this? Ah, damn thy priestly vows,
The which no man may dare to contravene;   55
For cryptic warning only may thou give,
If warning truly be what these words are.
If I did hear aright, some dire peril
Faceth now the queen, so wisdom caution
Doth suggest, and will I therefore this night   60
Keep careful watch upon her door. Perhaps
'Tis nothing; but perhaps 'tis not.

            (*Exit* CLAUDIUS)

SCENE 5

> *Elsinore. A passage outside the Queen's bedchamber. Enter* CLAUDIUS, *armed with a dagger.*

CLAUDIUS
She hath retir'd, and knows not that I watch,
For I would not alarm her with my fears;
Perhaps the priest was wrong, or I misheard,
And 'tis no danger here but in my mind;
I hope 'tis so. And meanwhile I will watch;   5
My post I'll keep behind the arras there,
For to be overcautious better is,
Than fear ignore, and find that thou dost err.

> (CLAUDIUS *hides behind the arras. Enter an* ASSASSIN. *He removes a small, corked bottle from his pocket, looks at it, and replaces it. He looks around and sees nothing, then tries the door handle, which is locked. He takes a key from his pocket and unlocks the door. As the* ASSASSIN *reaches out ot open the door,* CLAUDIUS *comes from behind the arras. He grabs the* ASSASSIN *from behind, pulling his away from the door, with the dagger at his throat.*)

CLAUDIUS (CONT'D)
Well, fellow, what's your business here?

ASSASSIN
I am but lost. What means this threat?   10

CLAUDIUS
You are lost indeed, sir, an' you lie to me.

ASSASSIN
I am a stranger here, my Lord. The castle halls are long; I know them not.

CLAUDIUS
Stranger, say you?

ASSASSIN
Aye, my Lord.   15

CLAUDIUS
If you are stranger here, why call me 'Lord?' Know you who I am?

ASSASSIN

In truth, my Lord, not so. But he who holds a dagger to my throat, I'll call him lord.

CLAUDIUS

How come you, then, to have this chamber's key? 20

ASSASSIN

The key, my Lord, will open many locks. I merely sought the seat of ease.

CLAUDIUS

We are not so inhospitable, sirrah, as to keep such places locked. I think you are a burglar.

ASSASSIN

O, no, my Lord. I am a physician.

CLAUDIUS

And is it medicine you carry with you in your pocket? Some beneficial remedy in that small, brown bottle? 25

ASSASSIN

Ay, my Lord, it is. An elixir of Turkey land, the cure for many ills.

CLAUDIUS

If that be so, then drink it.

ASSASSIN

I do not, my Lord, suffer from such malady as those it cures. It would not help me.

CLAUDIUS

Not so, my friend, I think your cure is there. 30 Tell me, am I wrong? Does this not cure the maladay that we call life? And did you mean to cure the queen of hers? This is her chamber, as I think you know. 35

ASSASSIN

Then I am most certainly lost. I said before, my quest was for the seat of ease, the which I feel a strong need to employ.

CLAUDIUS

Well, sirrah, come with me. I'll take you to a place where we shall loosen up your bowels. Your tongue as well, I think. 40

(Exeunt)

SCENE 6

Elsinore, the next day. The throne room. Enter KING HAMLET, CLAUDIUS, POLONIUS, *and* OPHELIA.

KING HAMLET
Where is the queen? 'Tis nearly noon, we see,
And she's not here.

POLONIUS
      I do not know, my Lord;
I have not seen her yet this fair, fine day.

KING HAMLET
We worry that she is not yet abroad,
For she complain'd of feeling ill last night,   5
Perhaps of fever, so she thought, and then
To bed to rest. Perhaps we should enquire?

POLONIUS
My daughter can, my Lord, enquire of her.

KING HAMLET
Ay, Ophelia, hie thee to her chamber,
Recall to her the time is growing late,   10
The servants soon will have the table set.

OPHELIA
I shall, my Lord.

(Exit OPHELIA*)*

KING HAMLET
We fear the queen is ill; she hath been from
Herself of recent weeks.

POLONIUS
      Hath she, my Lord?

KING HAMLET
Though she conceal it, yet she hath been ill.   15

CLAUDIUS
She hides it well, dear brother; yesterday
I saw her, but then noted nothing ill.

King Hamlet
She fears to let her illness become known,
Lest that our subjects should grow sad before
There's reason. Greatly do we fear for her,   20
For she is our life.

Claudius
Then hope thy life's prolonged.

King Hamlet
     I can but hope.

(Enter Gertrude *with* Ophelia*)*

Gertrude
Your pardon, good my Lord, I overslept.

Ophelia
I met her in the hall, my Lord.

King Hamlet
     How now,
My dear, art well?

Gertrude
     My Lord, all's well with me,   25
I did but over-sleep because my maid,
Who may, indeed, be ill, woke not herself,
Therefore she woke me not as well, and still
She slumbers, nor will she awake.

King Hamlet
     'Tis now   30
Quite near the noon hour, and within the hall
Our dinner waits. Polonius, go thou,
Fetch hither our physician, send him
To the queen's chamber, and see to her maid.
The rest, our meal awaits us in the hall.   35

(Exeunt all but Claudius*)*

Claudius
So, brother, had I known not where to look,
Forewarn'd of what thou did'st expect to see,
I should have miss'd the shock upon thy face,
When, seeing gentle Gertrude enter here;

Thou couldst not quite disguise thy great surprise   40
To see she liv'd, when thou hadst thought her dead.
That fellow thou didst pay to take her life,
Was not so staunch in hiding of his task
Once I had him convey'd to deepest cell,
And show'd him what his silence would produce.   45
                (*Takes out poison bottle*)
A cure, he call'd this, when I first did ask,
And, as I thought, a cure for life it is,
A most effective poison, so he said.
Well, he will speak no more, as now he lies
Asleep beneath the waters of the sound,   50
And would that I could sleep as peacefully,
Knowing what is right, and knowing, too,
That what is right to do is quite as wrong,
As any wrong the other would have done.
My course is clear, for I would have her live,   55
Yet clear 'tis not in any way at all;
If I would have her live, then he must die,
And doubly damn'd am I to take him off,
For he is both my brother and my king,
And both I should protect e'en with my life;   60
Nor dare I say to her, this hath he tried,
She knoweth not, nor will he tell her so,
For what he's done proclaims it secret strict.
He wishes she were dead, and will, I think,
Continue on until he reach that goal;   65
Therefore must I act to save her life,
Though hope of heaven yield to fire eterne.
           (*Exit*)

SCENE 7

> *Elsinore. The castle garden. Enter* KING
> HAMLET. *He lies down on a bench to nap.
> When the King is asleep, enter* CLAUDIUS, *who
> takes the bottle of poison from his pocket.*

CLAUDIUS

By this alone, can I insure thy life,
O, dearest Gertrude, though in hell I burn
For all eternity in consequence;
For thee, and for no other cause, would I,
Being damn'd and damn'd again, thy life preserve.   5

> (CLAUDIUS *pours the poison into the King's ear. After
> a moment, the King reacts, falling off the bench onto the
> stage. He tries to rise, but is unable to get to his feet, his
> strength already ebbing.*)

KING HAMLET

What is this? Wherefore lie I here in pain,
And lack the strength to get me to my feet?
Brother? What hast thou done?

CLAUDIUS

          Nothing, my Lord,
Except return to thee that which was thine,
The which, thou gavest unto one to give   10
Unto the queen, which I recovered
Of him, and at the third degree he told,
Who gave it him, and what he gave it for.
Therefore, lest thou conspire a new attempt,
I give it back to thee, and her her life.   15

KING HAMLET

I will kill thee!

CLAUDIUS

          I doubt it not. Or try.
That fellow which thou hiréd for the task,
That same foul man of Kolding who hath kill'd,
By his own word some nine and thirty souls,
Was very clear in telling of this juice   20
Which was distilléd for his craft, that first,
When it be pour'd into the ear, at once

It stealeth all the victim's strength; and then,
Within the sixth part of an hour he dies.

     King Hamlet
Yet shall I be revengéd upon thee.   25

     Claudius
I think it not. Three things shall come of this:
Thou shalt be dead, thy son shall then be king,
And Gertrude shall no longer fear her life.

     King Hamlet
Hamlet shall not be king.

     Claudius
     When thou art dead,
He shall.

     King Hamlet
   Never believe it. Dost thou think,   30
Dear brother, I know not that he be thine?
My will contains a sealéd codicil,
That should I die without recalling it,
Declares him bastard ere the council votes,
And being bastard he can not be king.   35
'Twas my intent, when age did take my strength,
The codicil recall and pave his way;
Now shall it disclose what should be hid, disgrace
His mother, disinherit him.

     Claudius
     Brother,
Thou art taken with thy trap; so instead   40
Thy throne shall come not to thy son, but now,
To him who follows second in the line,
That is, to me.

     King Hamlet
    Ambitious brother mine,
Thy colours now reveal in treachery.

     Claudius
Ambition did not prompt me to this deed,   45
But only to forestall thy treachery,
And save the life of her whom thou shouldst love;
If I am thus made king, so shall it be,

If Hamlet be my son and none of thine,
Still shall he reign in Denmark after me, 50
So I will marry with his mother dear,
And in the wedding him legitimate.

KING HAMLET

I shall have my revenge on thee, brother,
Though from the grave I must arise.

CLAUDIUS
                The dead
Are dead, and cannot harm who live, and thou, 55
Dear brother, soon shall join the harmless souls.

KING HAMLET

Yet shall I rise and murder thee, and with
Thy hope beside.

(KING HAMLET dies)

CLAUDIUS
            I think thou art too late,
Unless thou mean to rise up from the grave,
And cause some mischief from the spirit realm, 60
The which I do not fear, for God is just;
Nor will he sanction thee to have revenge,
When thou art justly kill'd to save the queen.
Now, brother, thou art dead; but how, and why?
Some reason must we show that thou didst die. 65
Aha! as sleeping in thy garden, thou
Wast bitten by an adder on thy hand!
                (CLAUDIUS takes out his dagger and pricks
                his brother's hand twice, lightly, to simulate a
                snake bite)
Now the alarm. Help! Help! The king! the king!

(Four GUARDS rush in)

FIRST GUARD
    What is't, my Lord! What's happen'd to the king?

CLAUDIUS

A serpent, I believe. It must have stung 70
Him as he slept; see, on his hand, the bite!

FIRST GUARD

What should we do, my Lord?

CLAUDIUS

The snake is gone, I saw it not myself,
But only where it stung, but he did say,
But moments ere he died, that it was so. 75
The four of thee, take up his body now,
And bear him off unto the central hall,
I to the queen must bear the tragic news,
And then the Council also must inform.

FIRST GUARD

We shall, my Lord. Take up the body. 80

(The four GUARDS *carry* KING HAMLET *from the stage)*

CLAUDIUS

And now, dear Gertrude must I tell of this,
But never shall I speak of how, or why;
'Tis best she knoweth not, though for her sake
The deed was done, and through his death now do
I keep her safe; her tender heart would not, 85
Methinks, have ta'en his life for hers e'en though
No other course would keep her yet alive
Once Hamlet had embark'd upon his course.
Then to the Council, and if they have read
The codicil my brother gave to them, 90
Then must I take such steps as I may do,
To keep the contents secret and unknown,
Or, if they've read it not, to steal it then,
That it shall not then harm his legacy.

(Exit)

SCENE 8

Elsinore. A room in the castle. Enter CLAUDIUS *and* CHIEF COUNSELLOR)

CHIEF COUNSELLOR
My Lord, it shall be as thou wish it be.
The codicil have I in secret read,
And never shall the people know of it,
For all the Council are agreed in this,
That all be kept in strictest confidence. 5
Now, though by this the prince may not be king,
And thou art elevated in his place,
Still shall we keep the matter from the queen,
And from, indeed, all save our little group.

CLAUDIUS
What reason shall we give for this, my friend? 10
None must know of Hamlet's bastardy, which,
So mother church permits, shall be but brief,
Yet may they ask for what cause doth thou now
Pass over him, and give the crown to me?

CHIEF COUNSELLOR
At Wittenberg, my Lord, remains he now, 15
And though the notice was eight days ago,
By swiftest courier sent upon its way,
In ignorance for two or three days more
Must he be kept before he hears the news,
Which, knowing, two weeks more must pass before 20
He shall have journey'd back to here again.

CLAUDIUS
And what of this?

CHIEF COUNSELLOR
My Lord, young Fortinbras,
The son of that same king thy brother kill'd,
Now threatens to invade our land anew;
Such threat demands response, and of a king; 25
We cannot, then, be kingless for a month,
And so in consequence of this great threat,
The Council wisely chose to make thee king.

CLAUDIUS
So shall it be declar'd; this will we tell
Our people, young Hamlet, and his mother. 30

CHIEF COUNSELLOR
Perhaps the queen should know as well, my Lord?

CLAUDIUS
Not so; in her eyes must her son be still
Legitimate, and only kept from crown
By circumstance of distance, and of time.

CHIEF COUNSELLOR
And the other matter, my Lord?

CLAUDIUS
                      In time, 35
In shorter time than one perhaps might think
To mourn, we shall be wed; she hath agreed,
And as the bishop on the Council sits,
Hath read the codicil, and so agrees
My brother hath no issue of this match, 40
His widow may, indeed one could say must,
His brother wed under levirate law,
Which God hath put in place, the bishop says,
Anticipating just such circumstance.

CHIEF COUNSELLOR
Thou wilt not tell the prince? 45

CLAUDIUS
                  Nay, best, I think,
To keep the truth from all.

                (Exeunt)

SCENE 9

A room in POLONIUS' *house. Enter* HAMLET *and* OPHELIA.

OPHELIA
Art thou very much disturbed, my Lord?

HAMLET
My father dead two months, and in an hour,
My mother to his brother shall be wed;
What madness is this in her, that she would,
When still in mourning black, throw off that gloom   5
That loving wife should feel for husband dear?

OPHELIA
I think she is in love, my Lord.

HAMLET
In love,
With husband's brother? Canst thou call this love?

OPHELIA
I can, my Lord.

HAMLET
Full fifty years is she,
Can woman love at such an age as that?   10

OPHELIA
My Lord, I doubt it not that she can love,
Age is no bar, the heart will have its say.

HAMLET
Being near my uncle she acts the child,
Her giddy giggles lack that dignity
Becoming to a woman of her age;   15
Thou lack'st two years of twenty, yet I see
The greater dignity in thee than she.

OPHELIA
They are in love, my Lord, and new-found love
Restores the old to youth.

HAMLET
How soon forgot,
Though, is my father, who this year should be   20

The only thought upon her widow's mind;
Hath he bewitch'd her, to forget her love?

OPHELIA

My Lord, of recent years thy time has much
Been spent in Germany, but here at court
Thou hast been absent much, and I do think, 25
Although thou like it not, the king and queen
Were not so close as ever they once were.

HAMLET

The bishop is to marry them, I'm told,
And hath his blessing given to them both,
When he should harshly call a halt to this, 30
Condemn as incest what they do propose,
For never brother married brother's wife,
Unless that wife be barren with the first.

OPHELIA

Thy uncle is the king now, so perhaps,
A king may do what others may do not. 35

HAMLET

Ay, how is that? My father was the king,
And now his brother reigns instead of me;
What made the Council to decide that way?

OPHELIA

My father, who doth know the Council well,
Related how the king did tell them 'nay,' 40
When first they did propose he take the throne,
But only with reluctance did accede,
As crisis loom'd, and thou wert far away.

HAMLET

And I shall back to school again, so soon
As I may leave; I would not linger here, 45
Within those castle walls, which should be mine,
Yet now my uncle shall possession take,
As she is jointress to my father's wealth.

OPHELIA

Thy uncle treats thee well.

HAMLET

          Too well, I think;
He treats me more as son than nephew now. 50

OPHELIA
He will thy father be, once they are wed.

HAMLET
I think it wrong.

OPHELIA
My father says he loves thee very much.

HAMLET
I had a father; one is all I need.

OPHELIA
My Lord, I see the pain upon thy brow,   55
I'ld take it from thee, if thou wilt allow.

(She embraces him. Enter LAERTES*)*

LAERTES
Well, sister, what is this?

OPHELIA
                The wedding preys
Upon the prince's soul, my brother dear,
Which all of us must shortly now attend.

HAMLET
Hast thou returnéd home as well, my friend?   60

LAERTES
I have, my Lord.

OPHELIA
              And now 'tis nearly time;
The wedding party doth await us all,
So churchward must we quickly wend our way.

LAERTES
For just such reason, Sister, was I sent
To fetch thee, at our father's beck, the prince,   65
As well, though others seek him out within
His chambers now.

HAMLET
              My mother may not wed,
It seems, without my presence there, so I
Must go at once, my seat in the cathedral

There to take, though I do wish it were not so, 70
And keeping from there, might forestall the day.

>   (*Exit* HAMLET)

LAERTES
Come, sister, father waits upon us now;
Some other time we'll speak of this as well.

>   (*Exeunt*)

SCENE 10

>   *Elsinore. The throne room, immediately after the wedding. Enter* HAMLET, POLONIUS, LAERTES, OPHELIA, GUARDS, *and* COURTIERS. *Enter to them* CLAUDIUS *and* GERTRUDE, *who speak to each other before they are presented to the court.*

GERTRUDE
How many years, I've long'd to see this day,
Which I did never think would ever be.

CLAUDIUS
Nor I, though I have lov'd thee from the time
When first I saw thee at thy father's side.

GERTRUDE
I told thee once that all these many years, 5
Thou wert the brother that I wished to have,
And now I have thee, so all things are right.

CLAUDIUS
Forever dost thou have me, dear my love.

POLONIUS
My honour'd Lords and Ladies, let me say,
'Tis my great honour to present this day, 10
This joyous day, this day when our new king,
Presents unto this gathered court, to thee,
Our much beloved queen who was, and now,
Is queen again.

Claudius
Though yet of Hamlet, our dear brother's death, 15
The memory be green, and that it us befitted
To bear our hearts in grief...

BLACKOUT

CURTAIN

BURYING DAD

CAST OF CHARACTERS

JOE, a retired Army General, mid-60s.
MARY, his sister, a teacher, two years younger.

SETTING

A visitation room at the Mortimer Funeral Home, today.

> *SETTING: The visitation room at Mortimer's Funeral Home. There is a closed, flag draped casket upstage, and a few folding chairs for visitors.*
> *AT RISE: JOE and MARY, two siblings in their 60s, are standing together. Their father is in the casket, and they are the only family members present.*

MARY

How many do you think will show up?

JOE

He had a lot of friends.

MARY

True.

JOE
Lots of friends.

MARY
The Morrises said they'd be here.

JOE
From next door?

MARY
When we were kids. Right.

JOE
He was a grouchy old jerk.

MARY
I thought you liked the Morrises.

JOE
I liked Suzy Morris. I never really cared for her parents.

MARY
Suzy was okay. Friendly.

JOE
Yeah. Friendly's good. She knew some interesting games.

MARY
Really?

JOE
Very interesting.

MARY
Like what?

JOE
Never mind, Sis.

MARY
I saw her last week, you know.

JOE
Did you?

MARY
She's put on a few pounds since we were young.

JOE

We all have.

MARY

I'd say about 200.

JOE

Ouch.

MARY

She didn't mention any games.

JOE

We were kids. She might not remember.

MARY

Maybe she doesn't want to.

JOE

Doesn't really matter.

MARY

I suppose not. Did we ever play any of those games?

JOE

Of course not. You're my sister.

MARY

Oh. Those games.

JOE

Those.

MARY

Sex games.

JOE

We were kids. We weren't even doing it right.

MARY

Probably just as well. What if her dad had found out?

JOE

You'd be here alone, because I'd be dead.

MARY

What about our dad?

JOE
After Suzy's dad killed me, he'd have killed him.

MARY
I mean if he was the one who found out.

JOE
I don't know. I could see him slapping me on the back, going, "Way to go, son, she's hot!"

MARY
Men.

JOE
I could also see him beating the shit out of me.

MARY
The beating's more likely.

JOE
Yeah, he could be a mean old bastard at time.

MARY
Parents were like that back then. Mom had her paddle and Dad had his belt.

JOE
I preferred the belt. He'd double it over so it made a lot of noise, but he didn't hit nearly as hard as Mom.

MARY
Well, Mom had to be pretty pissed off before she'd start hitting.

JOE
Parents could get away with a lot more back then.
(brief pause)
So could teachers. I got my ass whipped more than once in school.

MARY
Not any more. I'd get fired if I hit one of my students today.

JOE
Some of them, it might be worth the risk.

MARY
True.

JOE

We're avoiding the subject, aren't we?

MARY

What?

JOE

Dad. Our father's in that box over there, and we're talking about school, and paddling, and old neighbors and stuff.

MARY

What should we be talking about? Neither of us saw that much of him the last few years. Even when we did, did we really see him?

JOE

I suppose not.

MARY

He was there. He was breathing and talking. But it wasn't him any more, was it?

JOE

No.

MARY

Just as well Mom was gone before he got that way. Do you really think she could have coped?

JOE

Hard to tell. She coped with us.

MARY

Well, sure. She was our mother. She had to.

JOE

And she coped with Dad, too. I don't think he was the easiest guy to live with, even before he started losing it.

MARY

She loved him.

JOE

I guess.

MARY

Oh, she did.

JOE

He was still pretty grumpy and rigid most of the time.

MARY

It's that military thing.

JOE

What?

MARY

World War II. Discipline. Combat. Like that. You certainly know about that kind of thing.

JOE

Mary, he was in the Army for 18 months right at the end of World War II. He never even left the States. Hell, I did 30 years and never got that mean. Dad was just naturally grouchy.

MARY

He used to give you advice on your career. I remember that.

JOE

Most of it wasn't very good.

MARY

He meant well.

JOE

No doubt. But after a while it got annoying. I'd be in my office in the Pentagon, and my old man would call me up to tell me how I could advance my career.

MARY

He wanted you to get ahead.

JOE

I was the goddamn Chief of Staff. That's about as far as you can go without running for President.

MARY

Well, when you put it that way...

JOE

Here, someone's coming.

MARY

Be nice to them.

JOE

I'm always nice.

(Pause)

Who the hell are those people?

MARY

I don't know.

JOE

How many of Dad's friends do we actually know?

MARY

I'm not sure. Lots, should be. We use to know lots of them.

JOE

I remember the ones who were always around. The ones who showed up for the New Years parties, or came by on Christmas.

MARY

Sure.

JOE

The Richmonds, the Clarks, the Berneses, the Ottmans, and the Morrises. That bunch.

MARY

They won't be here. Except the Morrises. The rest are all dead.

JOE

Dad outlived most of his friends, didn't he?

MARY

I expect he made new ones.

JOE

So are these guys new ones?

MARY

No, I don't think they're coming in here. Looks like they're going into the chapel next door.

JOE

Warren, isn't it?

MARY

I think so. I didn't know her.

JOE
Busy place.

MARY
Three funerals today. You remember we used to make fun of Billy Mortimer? Kid living in a funeral home with all those dead people.

JOE
I actually thought that was kind of cool.

MARY
Yeah, well, you were kind of weird as a kid. You did all the big brother, protective stuff, but you were still weird.

JOE
I wasn't weird, I was cool. Ghoulardi blew up one of my model cars on his show. You couldn't get much cooler than that!

MARY
Oh, sure you couldn't.

JOE
It was you and the other girls used to pick on Billy. Most of us guys thought it was pretty neat, living in a funeral home. He told some great ghost stories about this place. There's this old lady who haunts the embalming room, because no one's been able to convince her she'd dead. And there's the liver story.

MARY
Every funeral home in the country has the liver story.

JOE
The old ghost lady is supposed to be true.

MARY
Think it is?

JOE
Nah, he probably just made it up. Or maybe his father made it up. We were kids when he told it to us.

MARY
Well, he owns the place now. Seems to be doing okay.

JOE
Yeah. Seems to. So do you think anyone is coming?

MARY

The Morrises.

JOE
(Checking his watch.)
I'm starting to wonder about them. It's nearly time to go to the cemetery.

MARY

They said they'd be here.

JOE

They're nearly as old as Dad. Maybe they changed their minds. Hell, maybe they both dropped dead themselves.

MARY

I doubt it.

JOE

Nobody here from the home, I suppose?

MARY

If they're in that home, they probably can't get around very well. I doubt we'll see anyone.

JOE

There's the staff.

MARY

I don't think they liked him very much. I'm pretty sure some of them didn't like him at all.

JOE

They're supposed to. We certainly paid them enough to take care of him.

MARY

They said he was hard to get along with.

JOE

He was that. Even before he lost himself.

MARY

One of the nurses said every time she'd come into his room he'd pull out his dick and ask her for a blow job.

JOE

What a gentleman.

MARY
Every time, she said. After a few times, she said she'd only go in there with one of the male attendants.

JOE
That take care of the problem?

MARY
Apparently not.

JOE
Was she hot?

MARY
I suppose, but why should that matter?

JOE
It doesn't for Dad. But, you know, I'm single again.

MARY
Looking for number five, are you?

JOE
I really thought it was going to work.

MARY
And what happened?

JOE
(Sheepish)
She, uh, ran off with another woman.

MARY
You married a lesbian.

JOE
Yeah.

MARY
Again.

JOE
Uh huh.

MARY
You married four lesbians. In a row.

JOE

They were hot.

MARY

They were strippers.

JOE

Strippers can be hot. Strippers are usually hot.

MARY

And all four of them ultimately decided they liked girls better than they liked you.

JOE

Okay, fine, call me Liza, if it makes you feel better.

MARY

Maybe you should have married Suzy. She seems to still be straight.

JOE

According to what you said before, she also weighs about 300 pounds.

MARY

Just don't marry any more strippers, okay?

JOE

I'll try not to. I'm getting too old for that anyway.

MARY

I didn't think guys ever got too old for strippers.

JOE

We never lose the esthetic appreciation. It's just that after a certain point in life, you start to realize that those naked college girls are really struggling to pretend they're interested in you.

MARY

I do have a couple friends who might be looking.

JOE

I'll think about it.

MARY

Hey, that old guy might be coming in here. No. Damn.

JOE

I'm starting to think we should have just skipped this part and gone straight to the cemetery. The casket's closed anyway; it's not like anyone is getting a last look at the old goat.

MARY

You may be right.

JOE

No one's coming.

MARY

I suppose all his friends really are dead.

JOE

Or he managed to piss all of them off before he died.

MARY

Even Dad couldn't alienate everyone. No matter how hard he tried.

JOE

Don't be so sure. There were those stories he liked to tell.

MARY

Some of those were pretty good.

JOE

The first time, sure. But he'd keep forgetting he told you, and then he'd tell them again. And again, and again, and again.

MARY

He did do that, didn't he?

JOE

The last time I went out with him, we were at this dance club he liked, and he introduced me to a couple sitting at the same table.

MARY

That was nice.

JOE

Five times. He'd forget, and keep doing it over again.

MARY

He was our father.

JOE

True.

MARY

He was an asshole, but he was our father.

JOE
He was senile. Well, first he was a grouchy bastard, and then he was a senile grouchy bastard.

MARY
That nurse wasn't the only one he ever waggled his dick at, you know.

JOE
What?

MARY
He tried that with me, too. Here, Baby, look at this big thing. Why don't you come over here and suck it for Daddy?

JOE
Jeeze. Well, he probably forgot you were his daughter. He couldn't remember who I was the last time I saw him.

MARY
I was 16. Believe me, he knew who I was.

JOE
Why the hell didn't I ever hear about this?

MARY
Because I knew you well enough to know you'd probably have killed him, and I didn't want my big brother going to jail. Anyway, you were off at West Point then.

JOE
So our father... with you?

MARY
No, but he obviously wanted to.

JOE
You never even gave a clue.

MARY
It only happened once.

JOE
So you managed to discourage him?

MARY
I kicked him in the balls. He decided to behave himself after that.

JOE

I can see why that would work.

MARY

As long as he behaved, I didn't see any reason to tell anyone.

JOE

Mom never figured it out?

MARY

I don't think so. I did make sure he was never alone with any of my friends, though.

JOE

Sensible.

MARY

Or any of our girl cousins. I just never could trust him after he tried that.

JOE

I wouldn't have.
(Pause)
He really was an asshole, wasn't he?

MARY

Mom loved him.

JOE

And you never told her?

MARY

No. I think it took me about ten years of therapy after college to even completely convince myself it wasn't partly my fault. You tend to think that, you know. Wonder what you did to make him do that.

JOE

You didn't do anything. He was just an asshole. We had the same problem when we eliminated the Women's Army Corps and integrated the women into the regular Army. There'd be a problem, and too many of the COs wanted to blame the woman for just being there, instead of blaming the bastard who'd attacked her.

MARY

Well, he's dead now. I suppose we should just bury him and be done with it.

JOE

No one's coming. Not even the Morrises.

MARY

Doesn't look like it.

JOE

He really didn't have any friends.

MARY

Most of them are dead now.

JOE

No, I mean I don't think he ever had any friends. Mom had lots of friends, and Dad got to tag along. That's all. They were her friends, not his.

MARY
(Looks at her watch)

It's about time anyway. I'll go find Billy and we'll get him to the cemetery and get this over with.

(MARY turns to look at her father's casket for a moment, then goes out, leaving JOE alone on stage. He walks to the casket, stands there in silence.)

(Blackout.)

IT'S THE COMPUTER'S FAULT

Cast of Characters
Rod, male, psycho, twenties
Lucy, waitress, late teens

> SETTING: *A nondescript room in* Rod's *house. One window, with shade drawn. A desk with a computer and chair. Another chair in the middle of the room.*
> AT RISE: Lucy *is seated in the chair, bound and gagged.* Rod *is pacing as he talks to her.*

Rod

I wish you weren't here. I didn't want to do this. Honestly. You seem nice. I guess. We haven't really talked, have we? I guess I should apologize for that, but I'm afraid you'd scream, or yell for help, if I took the gag off. I know I would. I don't like loud noises. Screaming bothers me. There are no neighbors, not for miles, but I wouldn't want to hear you screaming. I know what I have to do, but if you started screaming I'd get upset and have to do it quicker.

You wouldn't want that, would you? I mean, I'm sure you know what's going to happen, but why rush it, huh? You want to live as long as you can, right? I have to kill you, but I don't have to do it right now.

I suppose you're wondering why. I have to, you see. My computer over there, it says I have to. I took one of those quizzes. You know the kind I mean. "What famous person should you be?" That one. It asks you a lot of silly questions and you have to answer then. What's your favorite color. I said "blue," because blue was there. My favorite color is really indigo, but blue was the closest they had. I want to live in Paris, but that wasn't on the answer list, so I said New York instead. I'm sure it didn't make any difference.

Anyway, I took the quiz, and it said I should be Ed Gein. You know him? Know who he was? I didn't, but I looked him up. He was pretty odd. He killed some people, and they said sometimes he ate them after he killed them. You know, cut them up and fried them up on the stove. Someone said that. It was on the internet, so it has to be true, doesn't it? But you can see my dilemma. The doctor calls it Obsessive Compulsive Disorder. OCD. Like those crazy guys who wash their hands a couple hundred times a day.

No, I don't do that. I wash my hands when they're dirty, that's all. But I believe in the internet. That's how God tells you what to do. He puts it on the internet. He puts it in quizzes—in the results of quizzes. God wants me to be Ed Gein. And I saw you there, and you looked so tasty in that waitress uniform. Well, it was obvious, wasn't it? You looked tasty, and I was supposed to be Ed Gein, so naturally that was God telling me to eat you. I was supposed to kill you, and cut you up, and fry you up on the stove. I think fry. Maybe I'm supposed to make a stew? It'll be on the computer. If I put "cooking" into search, the first picture will tell me how to cook you, won't it?

It's funny, really. I don't usually eat girls. Not for supper, and not even the other way. You're a girl. I don't like girls that much. Not that way. But Ed did, I guess, and now I'm supposed to be him, but I'm still only going to eat you after you're cooked. None of that sex stuff. Ewww. Sex with a girl? Eww.

I'll try to make sure it doesn't hurt too much. Not like in that movie, where the guy kept the girl in a pit and wanted to fatten her up and make a suit out of her. Gein sort of did that. He made a girl suit, but I don't think he killed those girls. I think he just dug them up after they were already dead. Fattening a girl for her hide isn't nice. I'm just going to kill you, and cut you up, and fry some of you. Didn't Jack the Ripper eat a girl's kidney? Somebody ate a kidney. I like kidneys. And liver. I like liver, too. Kidneys and liver sort of taste almost alike, but just a little different. Some guys like one but not the other. I like both.

I should clean my hands. I'm not compulsive about that. Not at all. Never hurts to kill the germs, though. I wouldn't want to get any germs on you. You might catch something. What? Okay, I suppose that does sound silly, huh? I'm worried I might have germs on my hands and you'll catch something. I'm going to kill you, and I'm worried about your health.

I should worry about germs, though, shouldn't I? Not that you'll catch something from me, but that I might catch something from you. That would matter. You don't have anything contagious, do you? Something I should worry about? You look healthy, but how can you really tell? I'm not a doctor. What if I catch something from you?

You'd like that, wouldn't you? Give me some horrible disease that will come back to haunt me after you're dead. You're not really a very nice person, are you? Are you even a virgin? If I'm going to have you for supper, you really should be a virgin. The olive oil is. Fry a virgin in virgin olive oil. That just sounds right, doesn't it?

It does. It sounds just right. Don't you go disagreeing with me. I like symmetry. Virgin and virgin. Symmetrical. Are you a virgin? I don't see a wedding ring, so you're either a virgin or a slut. My mother warned me about sluts, about girls who go around screwing guys they're not married to. Before they're married. Whores. My mother warned me. Was it my mother? Maybe it was Ed's mother. It was somebody's mother.

You're very pretty. Did you know that? Well, sure. You'd know. Pretty girls always know they're pretty. I think I might even like you as a girlfriend. If I had a girlfriend. If I liked girls that way. My mother said I should have a girlfriend. That I should get a girlfriend. But what would I do with one? Girls are sort of icky—down there. You know you are. No, I like my friend Bobby. Bobby's not icky, not like a girl. Even a pretty girl. Bobby is nice. Bobby is very nice.

I need the hand sanitizer.

(Goes to desk and uses sanitizer.)

Are you comfortable? No? Do you think I should loosen the ropes? Why am I asking you? Of course you want them looser. Then maybe you could get out of them and run away. No point in that, dear. We're way out in the country. No neighbors for half a mile either way. No, you're going to die here. I can't let you get away, not if I'm going to be like Ed.

I guess I should get to it, huh? I know you want me to wait, but I'm getting hungry. I'm really sorry about this, but the quiz said I had to do this. It's not me. It's the quiz. The computer. It's the computer's fault. God talking to me through the computer, telling me I have to do this. I really am sorry. You were always nice when you waited on me. Never messed up my order or anything, and always friendly. Not like a lot of people in this miserable town. They just go, "Oh, look at the faggot. Look at the queer." Bastards. Well, screw them.

Hey, I'm sorry.

(Strangles her.)

I'm sorry. Really. I didn't have a choice. God told me I had to do this, told me I had to be like Ed. But now what? How do I cook you? I guess I should find out, huh?

(Sits down at the computer, typing for a few moments.)

Oh, a new quiz. Let's see. Uhm, yes. Loner, I suppose. Sure, I like helping people. I just helped that poor girl. She was never going to be rich or anything. Now she has nothing to ever worry about. Oh! They have indigo!

How cool. And Paris. Uhm, the first one is cuter. Definitely the kitty. And, okay, let's see what... Who's Albert Schweitzer?

                (Types. Looks over at the dead girl in the chair.)

Oh, damn.

       (Blackout)

Sunday Afternoon

CAST OF CHARACTERS
DAVE, male, mid-60s, middle class, healthy but early Alzheimer's
NORMA, female, mid-60s, Dave's wife
JUDY, female, about 40, their daughter.

SETTING
Dublin, Ohio. The present.

SETTING: A suburban living room at left. Sofa, matching recliners, console table, lamps. Pictures on the walls, fireplace, flat screen television over the mantle. This is the long-time home of a comfortable, upper middle class couple who have lived in it for many years. At right is the kitchen, with 1960s appliances and a linoleum topped, metal edged table and upholstered metal kitchen chairs.

AT RISE: DAVE is seated in the living room. NORMA is in the kitchen, talking on the phone and holding a produce bag full of turnips. She hangs up, leaves the turnips on the counter, and goes into the living room. Dave and Norma are in their mid 60s, casually dressed. They have been married for 45 years.

NORMA

Judy should be here soon.

DAVE

What?

NORMA

Judy. She's coming over this afternoon, remember?

DAVE

Oh. Good. Be nice to have her here. Been too long.

NORMA

Not that long.

DAVE

Couple months, right?

NORMA

She was here last Thursday.

DAVE

I meant the kids.

NORMA

They were here two weeks ago. They're not coming today.

DAVE

Why not?

NORMA

They're with Jeff this weekend.

DAVE

Why isn't he coming?

NORMA

Because they've been divorced for five years. They don't go places together any more.

DAVE

They got divorced?

NORMA

Yes. Five years ago.

DAVE

How'd that happen?

NORMA

They just fell out of love, I suppose. It happens.

DAVE

Didn't happen to us.

NORMA

Might have. I used to wonder if you were fooling around on me back when we were first married. Back when you were away in the Army.

DAVE

I was in Vietnam. I was too busy getting shot at to chase women. And there weren't any where I was anyway.

NORMA

It was hard for me to be sure of that. You heard all those stories about pretty little Vietnamese bar girls, looking to find themselves American husbands.

DAVE

There were no bars in the jungle, Norma. Just the NVA trying to kill us.

NORMA

Well, I didn't know that, and you weren't here with me, and we hadn't been married that long yet. If I hadn't had Mike to take care of I'm not sure I wouldn't have started looking around myself.

DAVE

I was drafted. I was only gone for two years. And the last six months I was at Ben Harrison, over by Indianapolis. I think I came home most weekends.

NORMA

You did. Then we had Judy.

DAVE

Got you knocked up real quick, didn't I?

NORMA

You sure did.

DAVE

I told you I never fooled around in Nam. Had to make up for lost time.
          (*Pause*)
Those were good days.

NORMA

Which? Nam or when you got out?

DAVE

When I got out. Even with a couple little kids running around you were a sexy thing back then.

NORMA

And I'm not now?

DAVE

I'm getting too damned old.

NORMA
(*Taking his hand*)
I don't get you hot any more?

DAVE

Sure you do. But then I forget.

NORMA

Right. You forget you're horny and fall asleep instead. That kind of thing makes me think you might be losing it.

DAVE

I'll never tell.

NORMA

If you were losing it, you couldn't tell.

DAVE

And if I'm not, I wouldn't. Confusing, ain't it?

NORMA

Sometimes I feel like I'm living in an old Warner Brothers cartoon.

DAVE

So who would that make me?

NORMA

Lately, I'm not sure.

DAVE

I think I want to be Rick. Then everybody'd come to my place.

NORMA

That was *Casablanca*. That was a movie, not a cartoon.

DAVE

Are you sure? I'm pretty sure I saw Humphrey Bogart working with Bugs Bunny one time. He was going to let Lauren Bacall eat him.

NORMA

How is it you can remember that, but you can't remember what I told you to get at the supermarket this morning?

DAVE

Cartoons are more fun than grocery shopping.

NORMA

I sent you for zucchini. You brought back a bag of turnips.

DAVE

Maybe I just don't like zucchini.

NORMA

You love zucchini. You eat it all the time.

DAVE

Doesn't mean I actually like it. Now acorn squash, there's something I really like. When you cut them in half and fill them with brown sugar and steam them in the oven.

NORMA

I never did that. Your mother did.

DAVE

Maybe you should start. It's delicious.

NORMA

Not today. We don't have any, and Judy doesn't like them. At least, I don't think she does.

DAVE

So what are we having?

NORMA

I don't know. Something easy. Hot dogs, maybe. Or we could just call the wing place.

DAVE

Get the hot ones.

NORMA

Judy likes the honey mustard better. So do I.

DAVE

So, get hot for me and honey mustard for you two.

NORMA

If we decide to order wings. It could still be hot dogs. Or maybe pizza.

DAVE

No, not pizza. They always cut it funny here. You call it pizza pie, right? So why do they cut it like a cake?

NORMA

We'll get something.

DAVE

Speedy Gonzales.

NORMA

What?

DAVE

That's who you'd be.

NORMA

Who I'd be?

DAVE

If you were a cartoon. You'd be Speedy Gonzales.

NORMA

I'd be a Mexican mouse? A *boy* mouse?

DAVE

You're peppy. We may be getting old, but you're still peppy.

NORMA

I suppose it's better than being Granny.

DAVE

You don't like canaries?

NORMA

I don't like black bombazine dresses, is what I don't like. Tweety's okay. I could be Tweety.

DAVE

Tweety's a boy.
    (*Pause*)
And you are granny, aren't you? I'm gramps and you're granny.

NORMA
Doesn't help me decide what to make for lunch. We're getting old, and we have grandchildren, but that doesn't help with menu planning.

DAVE
I could fire up the grill and cook burgers in the back yard.

NORMA
It's 18 degrees out there. Any cooking, we'll do in the kitchen.

DAVE
That cold?

NORMA
What do you expect in January?

DAVE
It's not summer?

NORMA
Only in Brazil.

DAVE
Did we ever go there?

NORMA
Where?

DAVE
Brazil. Did we ever go to Brazil?

NORMA
Why would we ever go to Brazil?

DAVE
Why not?

NORMA
Neither of us speak Portuguese, for one thing.

DAVE
We don't speak German, either, but we went to Bavaria that time. Looked at the castles. Mad King Ludwig's place. Or was it Baron Bomburst's?

NORMA
Who's that?

DAVE
I'm not sure. I just remember his name, and he lived in one of those castles.

NORMA
I never heard of him. I remember the castles, but not that guy.

DAVE
Well, it was Bavaria, and we saw the castles, didn't we?

NORMA
Sure. See Europe in ten days. Most of it on a bus with no air conditioning and too long between showers.

DAVE
You had fun, didn't you?

NORMA
Sure.

DAVE
Maybe we should do that again.

NORMA
We're too old.

DAVE
We did it before.

NORMA
We were 40 years younger, too.

DAVE
That long? I thought it was more recent.

NORMA
We went in 1973. We wanted to have more kids, and seeing Europe sounded romantic, so we left Mike and Judy with your folks and took off to Europe for a couple weeks.
                (*Pause*)
Worked, too. I was pregnant with Emily when we got back.

DAVE
Seems more recent.

NORMA
Well, it's not.

DAVE

This was before the kids were born?

NORMA

Before the last two, anyway.

DAVE

Oh.
(*Pause. Looks at his watch*)
Shouldn't we be eating soon?

NORMA

Not until Judy gets here.

DAVE

Is she coming?

NORMA

Yes, Dave, she's coming. That's why I sent you to the supermarket this morning to get stuff.

DAVE

You did?

NORMA

I did. You didn't get what I asked you to get, but I did send you there.

DAVE

(*Frustrated; a little angry*)
Why do you do this to me, Norma? You sent me to the store to get... to get... something. You sent me to the store, and you told me, Dave, bring home some... some... What the hell was it I was supposed to bring home?

NORMA

Zucchini. Other stuff, too, but mainly zucchini.

DAVE

Zucchini. You said, Dave, go get zucchini, so I got in the car and drove down to the store and looked around, and I thought, I don't actually like this stuff. I don't like zucchini, do I?

NORMA

You love zucchini.

DAVE

Well, I got there, and looked at it, and thought, I really don't like this stuff. It's slimy, is what it is. It's green, and it's slimy, and I don't like it at all. Not a bit.

NORMA

Dave...

DAVE

I don't like zucchini. Slimy green zucchini.

NORMA

You love zucchini. And it's not slimy. Whatever made you think zucchini was slimy?

DAVE

Over at the Henderson's last week. Slimy zucchini.

NORMA

That was okra. Okra's slimy, not zucchini.

DAVE

Long, skinny, green slimy stuff.

NORMA

Okra, Dave, not zucchini.

DAVE

Okra?

NORMA

Okra. The Hendersons are from Alabama. They eat okra. Collard greens. Chitterlings. Weird southern stuff like that.

DAVE

You're sure it's okra I don't like? Not zucchini?

NORMA

Yes.

DAVE

It just doesn't seem right. I go to the store to get... zucchini. But then I think, I don't like zucchini, but I do like it, I guess. It's okra I don't like. Skinny green vegetables. Why can't I remember which one I don't like? But that's why I came home with a bag of turnips. I like turnips. Always did, ever since I was a kid. Cut them up raw. Maybe put a little salt on them.

NORMA

No salt. Remember your blood pressure.

DAVE

Oh, yeah. I forgot about that, too! I'm getting to be an old man, so food's supposed to be tasteless!

NORMA

It's all right, Dave.

DAVE

Is it? You say Judy's coming with her kids, right?

NORMA

Not the kids. Just Judy.

DAVE

Did you tell me that?

NORMA

I told you that.

DAVE

Which one's the oldest? Why can't I remember which one's the oldest? She's got three kids, right, so one of them has to be the oldest. But I can't remember. Is Judy the oldest?

NORMA

She's older than her kids, certainly.

DAVE

No, I mean our oldest. No, of course she isn't. Mike is the oldest. Would have been our oldest. But he isn't any more. There's no Mike now, so Judy's the oldest, isn't she? Mike's dead, and Judy's next, so she's oldest now.

NORMA

Mike isn't dead.

DAVE

Of course he is.

NORMA

Mike lives in Detroit. He's a Michigan fan, but that doesn't mean he's dead.

DAVE

Then why don't we ever see him any more? If he isn't dead, why haven't we seen him lately?

NORMA

Because he lives in Detroit.

DAVE

We see Judy all the time. Why not Mike?

NORMA

Judy lives in Westerville. It's a twenty minute drive. It's more like ten hours for Mike.

DAVE

He still needs to come by more often if he isn't dead. How are we supposed to know he's not dead if he never comes by?

NORMA

He calls every week.

DAVE

Dead people can make phone calls. I saw that on the History Channel. It's something the space aliens set up.

NORMA

Mike's not dead. And there are no space aliens, either.

DAVE

Sure there are. What's his name said so. The shiny guy with the weird hair.

NORMA

The shiny guy with the weird hair is a nut who can't figure out how ancient people managed to do anything more complicated than kill a rabbit with a club, so he decides that aliens must have done it, and then goes on TV and convinces a lot of gullible people that their ancestors were too stupid to figure out how to build a stone wall.

DAVE

I think I need a beer.

NORMA

No, you don't.

DAVE

I do. And I need to know which of Judy's kids is the oldest, too.

NORMA

Mindy's the oldest.

DAVE

Mindy is?

NORMA

By five minutes. Then Bert, then Stanley.

DAVE

Which one is which? Which one wears glasses?

NORMA

Bert does.

DAVE

Oh, yeah. He's the smart one.

NORMA

He's the smart *looking* one. Usually all he really wants to do is play video games. Stanley's the one who always has a book open.

DAVE

Oh. What was I supposed to get at the store?

NORMA

Zucchini.

DAVE

Did I get it?

NORMA

No, you got turnips.

DAVE

Maybe I should go back.

NORMA

No. I told Judy to pick some up on her way over here.

DAVE

You don't want me to go back?

NORMA

If you did, you'd probably come back with a bag of onions.

DAVE

So write me a shopping list.

NORMA

I've been writing you shopping lists ever since we got married, and you always put them carefully in your pocket and never take them out again. I find them in your pocket when I take your jackets to the cleaners. So you never look at the lists, and you come home with the wrong stuff. Oh, you'd remember what I wanted, most of the time, but you'd always get all this other stuff, too. Stuff I didn't ask you to get, like those big bags of beef jerky.

DAVE

I like beef jerky.

NORMA

Too much salt. It's not good for you. Not any more.

DAVE
(*Suddenly very sentimental*)

You always take care of me.

NORMA

I try to.

DAVE

I could still go back to the store and get the... what was it?

NORMA

Zucchini. And I told you, Judy's bringing it.

DAVE

So you're going to make something with zucchini for lunch?

NORMA

I don't know what I'm making for lunch.

DAVE

How about a turkey?

NORMA

How about hot dogs?

DAVE

Why not a turkey?

NORMA

Because we don't have a turkey. And even if we did, it wouldn't be thawed. And it would take two or three hours to cook even if it was.

DAVE

I could go to the store, get a fresh one.

NORMA

No, Dave. How far is it to the store?

DAVE

I don't know. Half a mile?

NORMA

How long did it take you to go there this morning? How long to go to the store, buy a bag of turnips, and come home again?

DAVE

No idea.

NORMA

It took three hours. You got lost again, didn't you?

DAVE

I never get lost.

NORMA

Sure you do. You get lost all the time.
> (*Pause. She's been dreading having to say this.*)

I think maybe it's time you stopped driving. If you need to go somewhere we'll go together and I'll drive.

DAVE

I'm an excellent driver.

NORMA

That doesn't mean much if you can't remember where you're going.

DAVE

I'm going to the store.

NORMA

Not now. Judy should be here soon.

DAVE

We need to get all of our kids here soon. Have a little reunion.

NORMA

> (*To herself*)

That's what I'm afraid of.

DAVE

You say something?

NORMA

Just thinking out loud. Nothing important.

DAVE

Oh.

NORMA

Why don't you read something? Keep yourself busy. I need to do stuff in the kitchen now.

Dave

Okay.

(Dave *sits in his chair, taking a magazine from the rack beside it.* Norma *goes into the kitchen. Lights go up on kitchen, down on living room. In the kitchen, Norma paces as she talks to herself.*)

Norma

Dave, I love you, but sometimes... Why don't I want you to go back to the store? Because you'd get lost, that's why. And you'd forget what you're supposed to buy. Why you? Why not somebody else? Why not someone else's husband? Is that selfish? Let someone else's husband start forgetting things and not mine? Let you keep your mind and somebody else gets Alzheimer's? If that's what's happening to you. Is it? Are you getting senile? Or is it something they can fix? Circulation problems, like Em had a couple years back. She had those problem, and Carl took her to the right doctor and it was something in her arteries they could clean out and get the blood to her brain again. She's back to normal now. Is that your problem, too? Something a doctor can fix?

(*Pause*)

Or are you really losing it, and before long I'm going to have to watch you 24 hours a day? Make sure you don't just wander off into the woods and lose yourself. Or you say you're going to the supermarket and a week later I get a call from a cop in Omaha telling me they've found you there?

(*Pause*)

What am I going to do with you? What am I going to do with me? It's one thing if you die, but you're not going to do that, are you? You're going to live to be 90, and for way too much of that time it will just be your body here. It won't be you any more. He'll look like you, but he won't remember you. Even worse, he won't remember me. Can I handle that? Can I take having you forget me? You haven't said you love me in a week, and you always said that. Every day. First thing in the morning, last thing at night. Usually several times in between, too. How rare is that, Dave? Married for 45 years and you still tell me you love me all the time. Still say it and mean it! But now you don't, and I can't help but wonder... It's not that you've found someone else, dammit, it's that you're forgetting who I am. Forgetting that you love me.

(Norma *sits at the table, her head in her hands, not crying, but close to it. As she ponders, the back door opens and* Judy *enters, carrying a grocery bag. Judy looks taken aback as she sees her mother.* Norma *quickly stands, goes to embrace her daughter.*)

NORMA (CONT'D)

Well, look at you! It is so good to see you!

JUDY
(*Taking off her coat and hat and hanging them on the hooks by the back door.*)

You all right, Mom?

NORMA

Fine. I'm fine.

JUDY

You sure?

NORMA

Yes. I'm just fine.

JUDY

What's going on, Mom? Really.

NORMA
(*Indicating the bag*)

Is that the zucchini?

JUDY

Yes. But that's not what's going on here. Give.

NORMA

It is, you know. It's exactly what's going on here.

JUDY

What is?

NORMA

The zucchini. That's what's going on here. Do you know why I asked you to pick it up?

JUDY

I presumed you needed some and you were out.

NORMA

I did. I was. But do you know why I needed it?

JUDY

You ran out?

NORMA

Well, yes. But then I sent your dad to the store to get some this morning. It took him three hours.

JUDY
(This is worrying)
The store's a quarter mile from here. I used to walk there when I was a kid.

NORMA

Three hours. And then he comes home with a bag of turnips.

JUDY

Turnips?

NORMA

Turnips. He decided he didn't like zucchini because it's slimy.

JUDY

He's Italian, how can he not like... slimy?

NORMA

He managed to confuse zucchini with okra.

JUDY

Well, they're both green, but... Mom, I don't think I like the sound of this.

NORMA

He hasn't said he loves me since... when? A week ago yesterday, maybe? He always says he loves me.

JUDY

He's not...?

NORMA

No! No, he wouldn't. No, he just doesn't remember that he didn't say it. That's why it takes him three hours to go to the store and get the wrong stuff. He forgets where he's going, or how to get back. A little bit ago he couldn't remember which of your kids was born first, and I'm pretty sure he got Bert and Stanley mixed up. Oh, and he decided Mike must be dead, because he hasn't seen him recently.

JUDY

Has he been to a doctor?

NORMA

Yes. But the doctor wasn't positive. He thinks it's Alzheimer's, but he's not sure yet. I'm taking him again next week. He's getting worse, forgetting more stuff. He remembers stuff he did with his brother when they were kids, or things he did in Vietnam, but not what he did yesterday. How do you tell a man you've lived with for 45 years and loved for 50 that he's getting senile?

JUDY
I can't believe it's that, Mom. He's only, what, 67?

NORMA
Sixty-eight.

JUDY
Sixty-eight. People forget stuff as they get older. It doesn't mean they're getting senile.

NORMA
He's forgetting too much. It's not one of those things where you can't remember who was in some movie, and then later you do. Or you forget where you put your keys. No, he forgets how to get to the store, and all you do is turn right twice and you're there. Or he remembers we went to Bavaria and looked at all the castles, and then he thinks somebody called Baron Bomburst built one of them.

JUDY
(She knows who this is and it makes no sense at all)
Baron Bomburst?

NORMA
Yes. I remember mad King Ludwig, but who the hell is Baron Bomburst?

JUDY
Gert Frobe.

NORMA
Who?

JUDY
Gert Frobe. Goldfinger. He was the bad guy in *Chitty, Chitty, Bang Bang.*

NORMA
How did you remember that?

JUDY
I have three ten year olds. We've watched it about 40 times this year.

NORMA

Well, anyway, if he thinks a character from a movie is real, that's not a good sign, is it?

JUDY

I don't suppose.

NORMA

And it's just going to get worse.

JUDY

What are you going to do, Mom?

NORMA

See what the doctor says, I guess. I can't imagine being here without your dad. We've been married for 45 years, and we've slept in the same bed in the same bedroom for the last 42. Ever since we bought this place.

JUDY

It's got to be okay, Mom. It's Dad. He'll turn out to be okay. He has to.

NORMA

I hope you're right.

JUDY

Things work out.

NORMA

He knows, you know. He was talking about a family reunion a little while ago. I think he knows he's not going to be seeing all of you again. Or that he won't know it, more like.

JUDY

Are you talking about a home?

NORMA

I hope not.
(Long pause)
But it could come to that eventually.

(DAVE enters the kitchen)

DAVE

Where's my pipe?

NORMA

What pipe?

DAVE

The straight briar.

NORMA

Dave, you don't smoke.

DAVE

I'm pretty sure I do.

JUDY

Dad, you never smoked. Did you?

NORMA

He quit just before you were born.
(To Dave)
We threw all your pipes away back in the '70s. You don't smoke any more.

DAVE

I remember smoking.

NORMA

Not lately you don't.

DAVE

Feels like it.

JUDY

Dad, why do you think you smoke?

DAVE

I started smoking when I was 15.

NORMA

And you quit when you were 27. It's been 40 years since you smoked.

JUDY

Smoking's not good for you anyway.

DAVE

My father smoked. It didn't seem to hurt him any.

NORMA

No, not much. It just killed him, that's all.

DAVE

No it didn't. He's not dead.

NORMA

Dave, you think Mike is dead, and he isn't, and now you think your father is alive, and he's been dead for years. He died of lung cancer when he was Judy's age.

DAVE

How come you know this stuff? Why don't I know this stuff? I should know this stuff.

NORMA

Damned if I know.

DAVE

Your sure you haven't seen my pipe?

NORMA

You don't smoke.

DAVE

I know that. But where's my pipe?

NORMA

Why don't you look in the bedroom.

DAVE

Okay.

(DAVE *exits into the interior of the house.*)

JUDY

Just how long has he been like this?

NORMA

For a while. It's been creeping up on him, but lately it's getting a lot worse.

JUDY

I was here, what, two weeks ago? You said he was having some memory problems before. I know that. But before he always made sense, even if he couldn't remember everything. This is... I don't know. How do you suddenly think you smoke if you quit 40 years ago, or forget that your father is dead?

NORMA

Usually, when people come over, he gets better. Makes a special effort, I guess. But this has been coming on for a while now.

JUDY
You'd think I'd notice. I mean, I only see you guys every couple of weeks, so I ought to notice changes more. If you see people every day you might not notice, but you should if you don't see them that often.

NORMA
Maybe every other week isn't often enough to notice. Or maybe this is just a particularly bad day.

JUDY
I wonder if you really should be thinking about a home.

NORMA
So do I.

JUDY
Are you going to be able to handle him?

NORMA
So far.

JUDY
How much longer?

NORMA
That's what I don't know.

JUDY
You need to be thinking about it.

NORMA
I know.

JUDY
Have you looked into places? Some seem to be a lot better than others.

NORMA
Not yet. I don't really want to face this.

JUDY
You'll have to, sooner or later.

NORMA
I keep hoping it could be like Em Carson. You remember her.

JUDY
Used to live next door?

NORMA

Right. Then they moved to Florida. She was just like your dad, but it was a circulation problem. The doctors cleaned out an artery or something and she was okay again.

JUDY

Have you asked his doctor about that?

NORMA

He says that isn't it. He's not going to get better, just worse.

JUDY

Start looking at homes, Mom.

(Re-enter Dave, *carrying a two foot length of one inch iron pipe*)

DAVE

I found it.

NORMA

Found what? What is that?

DAVE

It's a pipe.

NORMA

What are you going to do with that?

DAVE

I'm not sure. I remember I was looking for it, and I found this in the basement.

JUDY

That wasn't attached to anything, was it, Dad?

DAVE

No. Just laying there on the workbench.

JUDY

That's good.

DAVE

I feel better now that I've found it.

NORMA

Why don't you go read something?

DAVE

I was going to go to the store. We're out of peanut butter.

NORMA

No, we're not.

DAVE

Are you sure?

NORMA

There are two full jars in the cupboard. And half a jar over there on the table.

DAVE

Oh. We need anything else?

NORMA

No, nothing.

DAVE

Oh.

(DAVE *starts to walk into the living room, pauses at the door, holding up the pipe*)

Uh, what's this for?

NORMA

I have no idea, Dave. You wanted it.

DAVE

Oh. Okay.

(DAVE *exits into the living room and sits in his chair, studying the piece of pipe*)

JUDY

You need to do something, Mom. I could get on the Internet and look up some places. See what people think of them.

NORMA

Do that when you get home. For now, how about helping me make lunch?

JUDY

Sure.

NORMA

There's time later to worry about your dad.

JUDY

If you say so, Mom.

NORMA

I do. For now.

(They start working on lunch.)

(Curtain)

www.ingramcontent.com/pod-product-compliance
Lightning Source LLC
Chambersburg PA
CBHW031406040426
42444CB00005B/437